Making the Most of your Garden

Ward Lock Limited · London

Richard Bisgrove

Making the Most of your Garden

Acknowledgements

Perhaps I should start by thanking Miss Hickmott not only for permission to photograph her garden but also for her convincing demonstration of how much can be achieved in a very small garden. Her garden in Devon is not much more than 6m (20ft) square and in two parts, separated by a drop of 4.5m (15ft)!

At the other end of the scale the National Trust deserve unlimited praise for their efforts to maintain many magnificent gardens during times of great financial uncertainty. Hidcote Manor is Mecca to many enthusiasts but Killerton also shows the influence of Graham Thomas' masterly hand. Tintinhull, Barrington Court and Knightshayes Court also illustrate this book but the last two in particular are still developing under the guidance of their creators.

The Royal Horticultural Society shares with the National Trust the responsibility for some gardens including Hidcote, but Wisley is the acknowledged centre of R.H.S. activities. The Society and the Director of Wisley deserve considerable praise for the continued development of the garden. Even those changes brought about for economy are usually changes for the better, making Wisley more of a garden without reducing the vast wealth of plants grown there.

I have recently had the opportunity of visiting many private gardens, each of which provided new ideas and inspiration. Mrs Todhunter created the shrub-rose border illustrated early in the book. Roy Elliott provided the idea and illustration for the combination of iris and tulip, and Mrs Spilman the four-year-old garden illustrated. The view of the fruit and flower-bordered vegetable garden is from The Priory, Beech Hill. The gardens around each of the fragments illustrated made my own efforts look pitiful, especially when one considers that Mrs Spilman's garden was started on a bare, windy hillside when (she would not mind my divulging her age I am sure) she was past three score years and ten.

However, lest it be thought that I write only as a visitor of gardens, may I next thank the University of Reading in its collective wisdom for maintaining Shinfield Grange and its garden. This unique resource among English universities is an inestimable asset in my work. Alan Hayes is head gardener: without his energy and contagious enthusiasm it would not be possible to maintain and develop the garden with our present small staff. The illustration of hemerocallis and *Campanula lactiflora* is his photograph of his idea, and the illustrations of the winter scene, Sorbus 'Joseph Rock' and Cheiranthus 'Harpur Crewe' are also his.

Otherwise the illustrations are mine, for better or worse. Although gardening is a subject in which practical experience counts above all else it is no coincidence that good gardeners so often have good libraries. Space limitations demand that I mention here only those books referred to in the text which are John Brookes *Room Outside* (Thames and Hudson, 1969), Christopher Lloyd *Clematis* (Country Life, 1965) and his *Mixed Border* (Collingridge, 1957). If a few extra words escape the editor's scissors I must mention that my most frequently consulted book is Graham Thomas' *Ground Cover Plants* (Dent, 1970) for the marvellous illustrations of plant groupings as much as for the invaluable plant lists.

Finally, and only because finality adds emphasis, thanks go to my wife for her patience in tolerating the garden almost as my second spouse, and to our children for teaching me the true purpose of a garden.

© Richard Bisgrove 1976

ISBN 0 7063 5136 3

First published in Great Britain 1976 by Ward Lock Limited, 116 Baker Street, London WIM 2BB

House editor Roger Grounds
Designed by Tony Cantale

Text filmset in Garamond by Servis Filmsetting Limited, Manchester Printed and bound by Leefung Asco Printers, Hong Kong

Contents

Part One

By Way of Introduction

Chapter I

Prologue

'MAKING the Most of Your Garden' is written not only for young people who find themselves owning a garden for the first time but also for older people who have lived with a garden – often for some years – without knowing quite what to do with it but with a nagging suspicion that it could be much better than it is. It will not, however, tell you how to avoid gardening nor how to undertake the basic techniques of gardening such as digging, planting and sowing, and for very good reasons.

That gardeners should ever be the authors of books on how to avoid gardening seems to me to be the height of dishonesty. Although this is a book about gardening, not about philosophy, I must express my belief that many of today's problems are caused by too much time to spare rather than too little. With time to dwell on our minor ills, misfortunes and other people's wealth it is not surprising that so many people are as unwell and unhappy as they appear to be. Gardening is the most fascinating endeavour imaginable;

it allows scope for individuality, self-expression, physical and mental effort and as great or as little a financial outlay as one chooses.

It is possible to create gardens which require the minimum of upkeep and some of this book is directed to saving of physical effort, not as a means of escaping from gardening but because saving of physical effort implies an increased requirement for mental effort thus exercising modern man's least used muscle, his head muscle. For the person who asks 'How can I do as little gardening as possible?' the quick answer must be 'Live in a flat or on a boat'. With a solidly negative outlook even the annual dusting of plastic plants around a concrete lawn would be too much effort.

But surely this is a fault of gardeners writing for would-be gardeners. There is some truth in supposing that clear instructions and labour-saving ideas might encourage the first-time gardener but this is only part truth. Presented with a mundane routine of pruning roses this week, sowing beans next week and mowing grass every week it

8

is not surprising that so many people want to avoid gardening. To do so without living in an overgrown jungle they invest in labour-saving gadgets and find the jobs becoming even duller and all their spare time devoted to tightening nuts, replacing washers and oiling all the so-called labour-saving devices.

This book, then, is almost a pre-gardening book rather than a gardening book. I hope to show you that garden-ing is not a mundane activity but a satisfying and relaxing way of life. By asking *what* you want of a garden rather than dictating *how* you should garden this week and the next you will be able to tailor *your* garden to suit *your* require-ments. Having decided *what* you want it is then an easy matter to find how to do it from the enormous mass of existing gardening literature of which perhaps the most useful publications are infor-mative catalogues. Catalogues are

Plants and space: a strong focal point separating 'here' from 'there' creates a sense of distance and space

usually free, they will answer most questions on how to sow, when to sow, what to sow, and what will survive in which soils and situations, but they are expensive to produce so please buy seeds and plants as well as acquiring catalogues!

The emphasis throughout the book is on ways of using plants (and especially on ways of using them together to create a long season of interest) rather than on plants to use, but first-time garden-owners should find the brevity of plant lists an advantage rather than a disadvantage. The book is selective rather than encyclopedic because there are already very good (and very large!) encyclopedias about bulbs, annuals, herbaceous plants and the other types of plant discussed here. As I live on one side of Reading with a garden of gravel over chalk and work on the other side with a garden on heavy clay the plants mentioned in the pages of this book can be relied upon to tolerate a wide range of soils unless noted to the contrary, and although not all of them are commonplace they can be obtained from most good nurserymen.

To sum up, this is a book written especially for the new or the reluctant gardener to introduce him to the jobs of gardening rather than to bore him with too many details before they are needed. Because it was written to encourage a positive and thoughtful approach to this most fascinating of subjects and to stimulate observation rather than provide pre-digested answers, I hope it will be of use to a wider circle including those who are already enthusiastic and experienced gardeners.

Chapter 2

What is a Good Garden?

THE first step in making the most of your garden is to decide what you want the most of. This may seem terribly facile, too obvious to need stating, but how many people stop to think *why* they have a garden? In case you are one of the many who do not read introductions, it is stated there that the purpose of this book is to ask *why*? as well as to explain *how*, for once you know why you want to do something it is much easier to decide how to do it – and there are innumerable books written to tell you how. Asking why you want a garden, then, is the first and one of the most important steps in designing your garden.

Many people regard 'Design' as the magical ability of a few lucky people to wave their pencils and produce gardens of enormous beauty in a tiny space. Others regard designers as impractical eggheads producing plans to adorn the pages of glossy magazines rather than gardens for their owners to live in and enjoy. In fact there is no magic in design: like most other tasks it involves a mixture of common sense, practice in the employment of a few basic techniques and a great deal of careful thought in the choice, positioning and association of the many pieces which together make a garden. Design includes both the logical process of surveying the garden as it exists and the creative effort of shaping the garden to include the many uses foreseen for it.

Good design, therefore, can be learned and a good design is essential to make the most of your garden. However, design is not merely making a garden look nice: it involves the tailoring of an individual plot of land to suit an individual person or family. Those who frown on the impracticalities of the glossy magazine designers usually fail to realize that the designer was working for someone else to produce that design and that the result would have been very different in other circumstances.

The first step, then, in making the most of your garden is to decide what you want to make the most of. Is the garden to be used for growing vegetables or exhibition chrysanthemums, to provide territorial rights for young

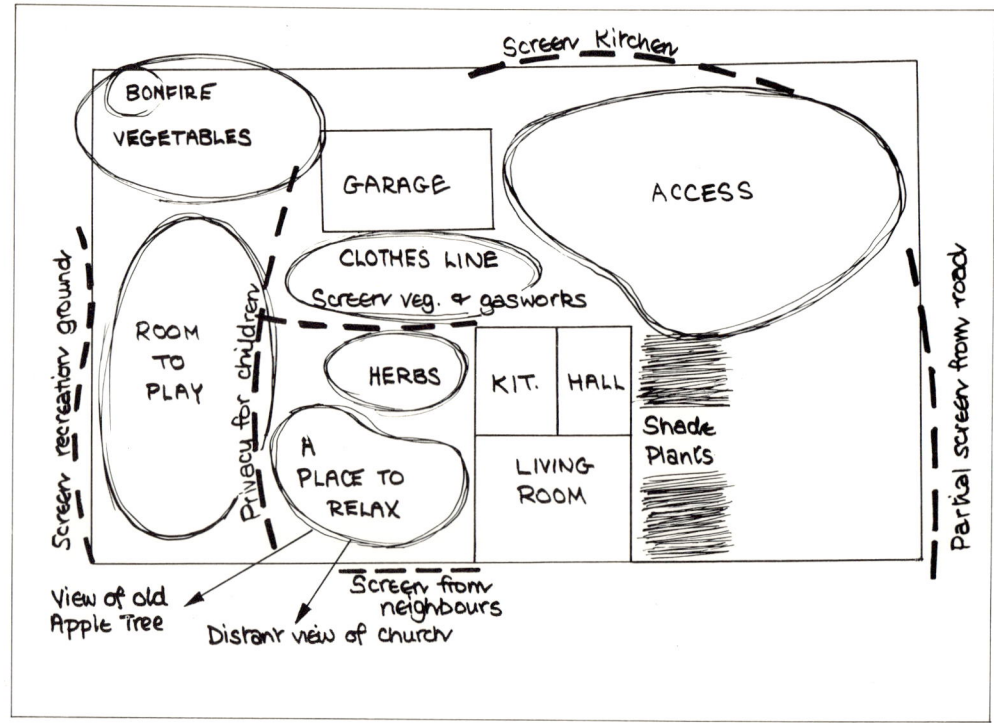

A preliminary garden plan: uses and views begin to give the garden its unique character

children or a sheltered haven for their weary parents, a place to dabble in plants on Saturday morning or to give a cocktail party on Saturday evening? Usually it is called upon to fulfil not one but several duties and it is important to decide which of these are most important if some compromise is necessary. Usually the most important consideration is that the garden should be attractive so we should look, first, at what makes it so. Even when appearance is not the primary purpose, as might be the case with the vegetable or exhibition flower grower, it would be unfortunate if, for the sake of a little extra care the vegetables or prize blooms were not grown in such a manner as to make the garden attractive as well as useful. Indeed, one of the great joys of

design is that so much can be achieved with a little thought: it is a basic understanding that the parts of a design should complement each other which means, in effect, that one and one often add up to much more than two!

When considering the whole garden it is not the colour, form or novelty of the individual features which matters – the rockeries, beds, sundials and fountains – so much as the sense of space, simplicity, variety and identity which the features together create.

Space

Space is not a well understood concept among gardeners nor is it one which is easy to talk about concisely. To hold forth on 'spatial structure' and 'spatial sequence' is reminiscent of the grandiose gestures of Tony Hancock when, with raising of eyes and sweeping of arms he pronounced his photography to be 'painting with light'. Nevertheless, if you consider what makes the gardens you visit attractive, it is not usually one particular plant or feature but the *surroundings*. Gardens are seen from within with a satisfying feeling of enclosure. If enclosure is lacking the garden seems bleak; if it is too pronounced it seems cramped, stifling. It is no coincidence that we speak of working *in* a garden but *on* an allotment.

Why, then, do so many people think of a garden as the patch of land around their house on which to grow plants? The answer, surely lies in our Victorian heritage. Until the latter half of the last century most gardens of which evidence remains were the work of professional 'landscape gardeners' and whether one views the plans of the Elizabethan gardens of the 17th century, the great landscape gardens of the 18th or the more elaborate creations of the early 19th the same techniques of orderly but varied division of the gardens into smaller spaces can be seen. As the 19th century progressed the financial fruits of the industrial revolution were distributed to more and more people, the population itself grew rapidly and large numbers of suburban dwellings each with its small garden came into being. Quite suddenly new gardens became sufficiently small that dividing them into still smaller spaces was obviously undesirable. However, even the smallest garden was surrounded by a sub-

stantial brick wall so the garden space was very clearly defined. Thus the rash of gardening journals which sprang up to advise the new garden owners, unable to afford the undivided attentions of a professional consultant, were able to concentrate their efforts on prescriptions for planting. Gradually the idea of the garden as a place to grow plants became universal and the journals devoted more and more of their printed page to singing the praises of bigger and better flowers. Simultaneously, of course, those precious garden walls were disappearing to be replaced by a strand of wire, split chestnut fencing or more recently chain link fencing which, although they serve to demark the boundaries, contribute nothing to the comfortable feeling of being *in* the garden.

Thus we arrive in the late twentieth century, when four out of five people have a garden and probably three of the four are looking for help to make the most of their garden, knowing that it is not a case for yet another rockery or rose bed but unable to decide precisely what is required.

What *is* required is a garden with a well defined structure, the walls, doors, ceilings, windows and floors of a building structure being analogous to background planting, openings, tree canopy, vistas and a ground plane of grass, paving or low ground-cover planting in gardens. Also as in buildings, the structure creates spaces, 'outdoor rooms' whose varying sizes and proportions give character to the garden.

13

This important idea receives much greater attention in Chapter 4 and it is useful to think in terms of space and structure when visiting other gardens. Although few of us have Stourheads or Hidcotes at our disposal, it is possible to characterize such gardens and to capture their essence in our own small domains whereas merely planting such specimens as appeal in the far larger settings of these gardens is doomed to failure.

As mentioned briefly above, it is the grouping of plants which creates a garden: a collection of individual plants more closely resembles an allotment.

Simplicity

The analogy between gardens and allotments can usefully be continued when discussing simplicity. Why is it that, however well cultivated allotments may be, several allotments together always look untidy? The main reason is that there are too many objects to look at: the sheds, heaps, bean poles and fruit cages of the various allotments are not related to each other, there is no clear pattern to unite the various elements so the scene causes visual indigestion. So in gardens, if each plant stands in splendid isolation there are too many features to be appreciated. Simplicity of design is more pleasing. This does not mean using only one or two species but ensuring that the plants' shapes blend one into another to form a smooth outline.

Another lesson to be learned from even casual observation of allotments,

Too many small features create a restless appearance which spoils the garden

although somewhat aside from the main point of the discussion, is that individual well-tended plots have a certain beauty which always results from good workmanship. It is the unused and untended areas – the unmown path edges, the fringes of the site and the occasional neglected plot – which cause offence. So in the garden it is the unused or unusable corners which detract from the garden and the appearance can be improved beyond measure by taking care that each part of the garden is put to full use in the preliminary design.

Variety

To call for variety may appear to contradict the need for simplicity but this is not so. Too much simplicity is bland, monotonous. The introduction of a focal point for interest enlivens the scene enormously, but, because the background plus the focal point form one composition, the simplicity is not impaired. Variety in small gardens results mainly from contrasts of form, texture and colour in plants. Without a simple background it is not possible to achieve this contrast: variety itself becomes monotonous and the garden looks untidy no matter how carefully tended. It is important, therefore, that focal points are recognized as such and kept rather few in number although, with the ever-changing nature of living plants, it is possible to design planting schemes with several focal points, each of which comes to the fore in its due season.

Smoothly rounded forms create a simple outline for a garden full of interest. Two straight borders flanking a straight path need not be dull!

Opposite:
Trees, shrubs,
climbers, herbaceous
plants, annuals and
tender perennials all
contribute to a long
season of colour in
this small garden

Identity

Each garden reflects (whether we like it or not!) the character of its owners and each, therefore is unique. It is important, however, that the garden bears not only the characters of its owners but also an atmosphere of its own.

In large gardens subdivided as they usually are into several spaces this identity is important to emphasize the coherence of the garden. The advantage of a large garden diminishes if it is made to look like a collection of little gardens. Coherent identity can be fostered by linking the spaces along vistas, by using focal points which can be seen from several of the spaces and by constant use of the same materials.

In small gardens character is more easily attained by the need to have a simple effect. Elimination of unnecessary changes in paving materials, concentration on a limited range of colours or plant types in the garden will result almost automatically in the garden taking on a recognizable character. It is still worth the extra mental effort, however, of checking on the choice of materials to ensure that all are compatible and that all reinforce the desired identity of the garden. Further emphasis is given to this in Chapter 5.

This, then, completes the first necessary step in making the most of your garden. The many purposes which the garden is to serve are considered and one is prepared to plan them in an attractive setting with a well defined spatial structure, having a simple but varied form.

Chapter 3

Positive Thinking

IN ADDITION to deciding what one wants the most of, the other important preliminary is to consider what there is to make the most of: the existing garden environment. Buildings (including of course the house itself), walls and fences, manholes, existing plants and other important factors such as soil quality, areas of sun and shade, wind directions, slopes, good and bad views will all provide clues as to the way in which the garden should develop. The soil, for example, will obviously influence the choice of plants for various purposes, as a garden of healthy plants is invariably more satisfying than one in which rarities are being cossetted in a miserable existence on unsuitable soils. There is nothing more depressing than gaunt, yellowing rhododendrons in their little peat-filled holes on chalky soil, or the wilting of a would-be bog garden on a gravelly hillside. Less obviously the soil may influence the whole form of the garden. On clay, drainage is usually a problem, grass is difficult to grow and unsuitable for walking on in winter so outdoor life more or less necessitates substantial areas of paving perhaps with most other flat areas being devoted to low planting – periwinkle *Vinca minor* or ivy *Hedera helix* – rather than lawn. On sand or chalk, a lawn can usually be walked on for most of the year and only the most used sitting areas and paths will need to be paved giving the garden a much more open appearance.

Slopes add interest to any garden, but whether the natural landform is combined with undulating groups of shrubs in a flowing composition or is levelled in a series of terraces will depend on the workability of the soil, the steepness and stability of the slope, the size of garden and the uses to which it will be put. The existence of good or bad views will determine whether one wants an outward or inward looking garden and even such small points as the position of manholes will have some effect. The worst place for manholes is in a lawn. They are better designed into a paving pattern or concealed in areas of planting but *not* half concealed by a plant or plant container which only draws attention

Opposite: Subdued lighting beneath a foliage canopy emphasizes the brilliance of flower-colour

to the position of the manhole and indeed really makes a feature of it.

Making the most of your garden implies a degree of optimism and it is very important in designing a garden to do so in a positive manner, to use existing features to the greatest advantage rather than to complain that a tree or manhole (or the house!) is in exactly the wrong position.

Because modern gardens are so small it is important to ensure that nothing detracts from their appearance. Many people ask how to hide sheds, manholes and other undesirable objects almost automatically just as our Victorian forbears sought to hide the legs of their tables. But screens are often uglier than the sheds they hide, and how much more obvious are manholes when they are supposedly concealed under an isolated trough at an odd angle in the middle of the lawn. It is much better to select well-designed garden buildings and to site them where they contribute to the garden scene, to fit manholes into a paving pattern or to incorporate them into large plantings where they can be effectively concealed.

In this context it is useful to remember that small garden buildings disrupt the garden scene not by their colour or materials but by their hard outlines. Planting trees or shrubs behind a shed to break the outline is much more satisfactory than planting in front in a vain attempt at concealment. Many people also regard the necessary intrusion of sheds, garages and greenhouses into gardens as unmitigated evils without realizing the advantages which such structures offer in giving height, and hence the all-important sense of enclosure, to small gardens. The extensive landscape gardens of the eighteenth century were regarded as living paintings to be viewed from the principal windows of the mansion but our twentieth century gardens are better thought of as extensions of the house, as architectural or sculptural compositions through which we can walk and in which we can live. With this point of view, then clearly the walls of buildings, fences and screens, can be combined to form the basis of the garden's permanent structure. Thus the ugly shed with a suitable backdrop (and if really necessary some camouflage) becomes an unexpected asset.

As well as providing structure, walls also deflect the wind and create shade or trap the sun's warmth depending on their orientation. This will determine where one can best sit to feel comfortably enclosed and sheltered while still receiving the welcome rays of the sun and where one sits will in turn decide where plants and other features are required to satisfy the eye. Thus the garden's form slowly and sensibly evolves. Wind is difficult to control in small gardens because it is deflected and funnelled by solid obstructions and gusts through any openings creating dust-laden eddies. Hedges, perforated screens and generous use of wall-plants filter the wind, absorb its energy and give much better shelter in most situations. Sun and shade, however, are

With its silhouette
softened by back-
ground planting a
garden building
becomes a pleasant
feature

much more predictable as there is a daily and seasonal cycle with which everyone is familiar. This predictability is very fortunate as sun and shade are immensely important in gardens from three points of view.

Firstly, of course, the degree of exposure to sunlight largely determines which plants can be grown successfully. Some woodland plants, especially ferns, will wilt and shrivel in full sun unless the atmosphere is very humid whereas many alpines, grey leaved plants and others become lank, fall prey to diseases and fail to flower in shaded situations.

Sun and shade are also important to the human occupants of the garden but humans, being rather fickle creatures, tend to require what is least available. In winter a sheltered corner which traps the few available rays of sun is greatly appreciated and it is surprising how often one can sit out for half an hour in January or February if the

Seasonal variations in the sun's daily cycle will influence the siting of many garden features

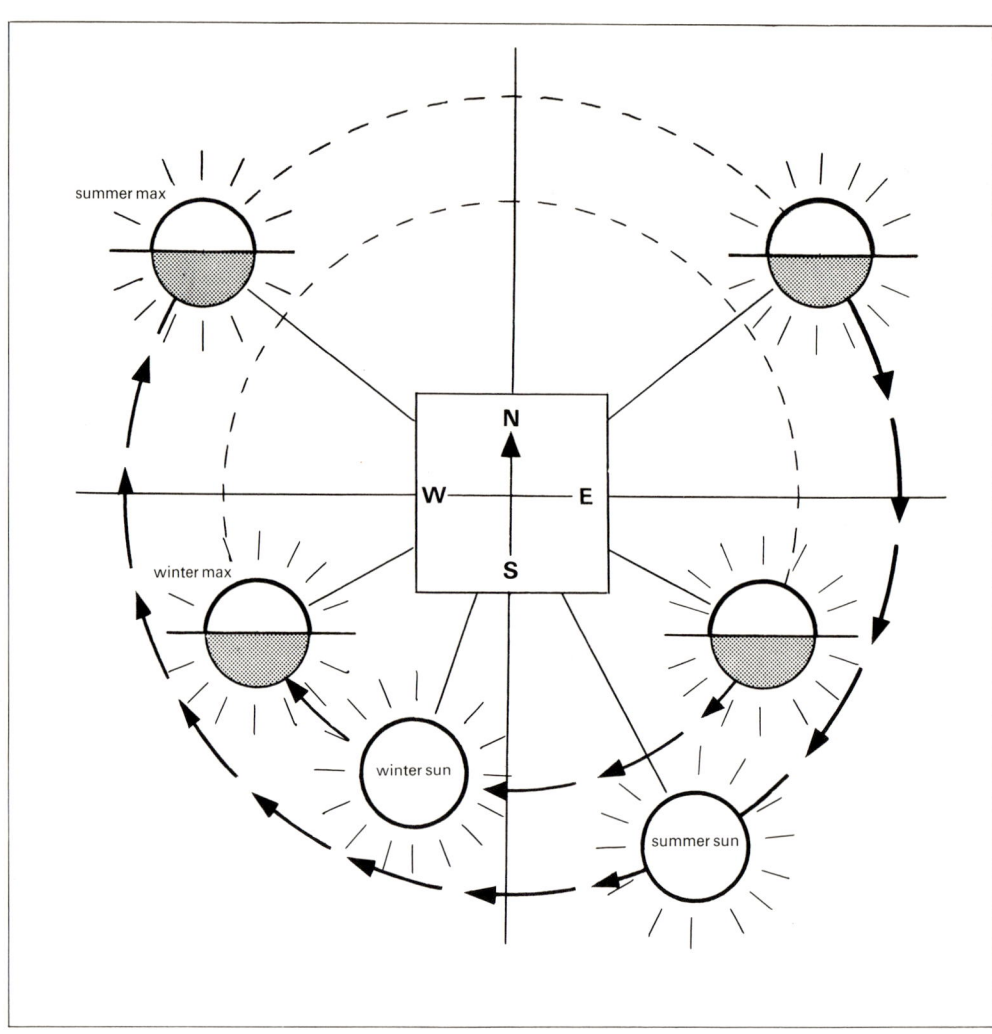

opportunity exists. In August, however, when sun is to be had in plenty, we wilt like delicate ferns and eagerly seek a shaded spot in which to collapse. Our climate being notoriously unpredictable, with some August days being colder than the warmest January days (or so it seems to our slowly adjusting bodies) any garden inhabited by people who enjoy being out of doors should be designed with a view to having a choice of sun or shade.

Beware though the simple assumption that a south-facing wall is sunny and a north-facing one shady. It is true that the south facing wall receives most sun (in the northern hemisphere) but conditions are not uniform throughout the day or the year. Generally speaking, the sun rises in the east and swings round in a southern arc to set in the west. In summer the angle through which it travels each day and the angle it reaches at midday are greater than in winter. In

mid-winter therefore it rises in the south-east, sets in the south-west and north facing walls receive no direct illumination. The sun-angle is low and shadows are about $2\frac{1}{2}$ times as long as the object creating the shadow is high. A two-storey house, therefore, would shade about fifty feet of the garden on its north side at midday. In summer, however, the sun rises in the north-east and sets in the north-west so north facing walls receive several hours of illumination in early morning and late evening. A south facing wall is in shade until 6–7 a.m. (depending on local time) and, more important for those anticipating sitting out on summer evenings amid the scent of jasmine, roses and other perfumes, it becomes shaded again after 6–7 p.m. Shadows are short, being less than half the height of the object creating shadow at midday so any part of the garden more than ten feet from a two-storey house would get sun for much of

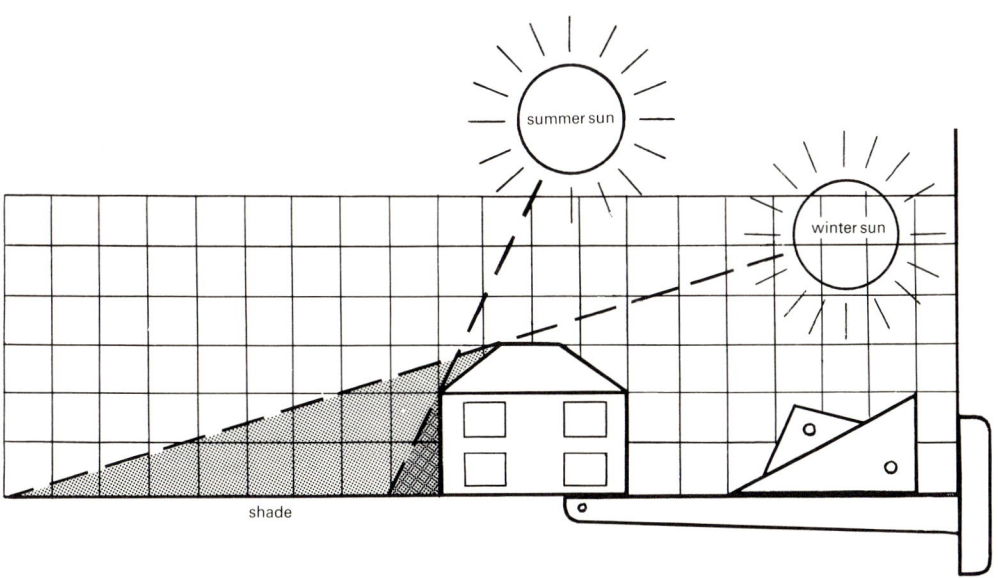

Sun angles and shadows vary throughout the year. This may determine the position of patios and other sheltered corners

the day, even on the north side. When the choice exists, therefore, and terraces are to be used mainly on the long summer evenings, it is wise to consider a west or even north aspect rather than automatically settle for the commonly recommended southern aspect. For brief winter forays, however, the sheltered south-west facing corner remains the counsel of perfection. When the main garden-front of the house faces due north there is often an expression of great dismay but such a layout has many advantages. In particular it allows the garden to be seen quite literally in its best light, because the third and in many ways most important aspect of light and shade in gardens concerns the illumination of plants.

The impression given by a garden depends, much more than we normally realize, on the quality of light which illuminates the garden. On a cold, grey November day it is not the garden which is bleak but the watery light which spreads bleakness over any scene. In spring the freshness of the garden is due in large part to the light which is clear but not yet strong. The same freshness can be seen in a summer garden if the intensity of light is reduced by viewing through sun-glasses or by shading the garden itself with a tree canopy. This effect of reducing the light intensity is, incidentally, why garden colours look so much richer on summer evenings than in the heat of the day. In many ways the small garden owner is at a distinct advantage in this respect, for when the small garden is enclosed, the enclosure necessarily restricts the view and, unless one lies on one's back in the middle of the garden, blots out much of the sky. The bleak grey light of winter and the strong white light of summer are unable therefore to impair the

The advantages of a north facing house

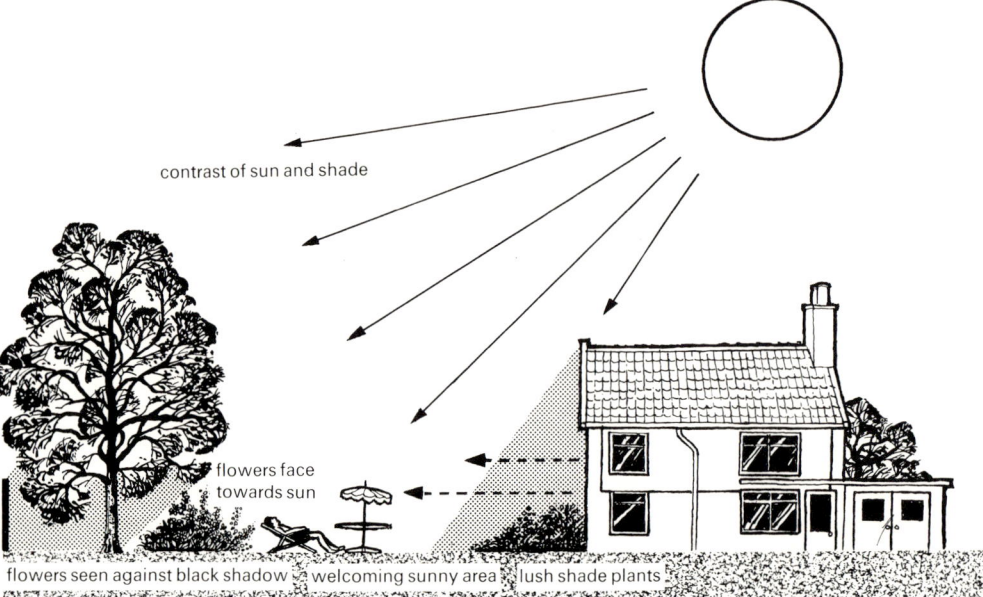

contrast of sun and shade

flowers face towards sun

flowers seen against black shadow   welcoming sunny area   lush shade plants brightness of the garden. The owner of a north-facing house is able to make best use of the natural illumination of his garden. The shapes and textures of the plants are emphasized by the contrast of sun and shadow instead of being presented as a flat surface without the sparkle of sunlight, many flowers turn towards the sun (daffodils, for example, and *Chrysanthemum uliginosum*) and all shrubs flower more freely on their sunny rather than their shady side. One also has the possibility, with a north-facing view, of the bold display of sun-lit flowers or bold plant form against the black background of tree shadows. Lastly, the whole union of house and garden can be strengthened by planting immediately outside the windows with the many lush, shade-tolerant plants available, even continuing the theme inside with maidenhair and other ferns. This provides a cool green frame for a view of the sunny sitting area at the far end of the garden, an attractive invitation to wander into the garden.

To recapitulate, the two important stages of garden design are the consideration of the purposes the garden is to fulfil and the examination of the existing character of the site. Buildings and fences can provide shelter, blot out unsightly views and give the garden a sense of height and enclosure; the soil, the rainfall and so on will limit the range of plants which can be well grown and will suggest how much of the garden should be paved, or planted, or left as open lawn; the pattern of sun and shade at various times of the day or the year will indicate suitable locations for sitting or for the greenhouse or vegetables, for the children's play equipment and thus the form of the garden gradually evolves in the way which best combines the requirements and existing features.

This, then, is design: not a magic ritual at the drawing table but a sensible process in which the features required of a garden are tailored to the available land and budget. It implies the thoughtful choice and grouping of materials, including plants, to form an attractive space, good workmanship in construction and care in maintenance. Constant physical or mental effort is not necessary but if anything is done in the garden it should be well done. The reward for this small effort is a garden improved out of all proportion from the scatterings of plants, sheds and ornaments which characterize so many new developments. Good design, then, is synonymous with making the most of your garden.

Part Two

Plants and Gardens

Chapter 4

Plants and Space

THE main form of the garden depends on the balance between open space and mass planting. An analogy can be drawn between the open space and planting of a garden on the one hand and the floors and walls of a building on the other, except that in the garden the distinction between the 'floor' and the 'walls' is usually much less obvious. In buildings rectangular blocks are piled one on another and there is a sharp contrast between the exactly horizontal floor and the exactly vertical walls; a garden is made of a single layer of generally rounded plants on an often irregular base, so horizontal and vertical blend subtly one into the other. Furthermore, in most gardens plants act as both the framework and the decorative contents so any distinction between walls, floors and furnishings is not obvious and the decorative attributes of the plants are emphasized at the expense of the garden's structure.

It is useful to think of the garden as an outdoor room not only in terms of its uses (as so ably expounded by John Brookes) but in terms of its structure, with low planting, paving and water forming the floor and tall planting, fences and buildings forming the walls, having strategically placed openings to admit light and reveal the view. In very small gardens the analogy is easily seen: the floor is mainly paved or of grass and surrounded by walls or fences, perhaps softened with climbers. In larger gardens walls and floors melt imperceptibly in undulating banks of planting but the structure is still important and the walls require the emphasis of additional height. Just how high the planting should be is not easily decided and even if one could decide on a precise height, making plants conform to the decision is far from easy, beginning as they do as very small objects and growing eventually to become embarrassingly large. However, as a very broad generalisation the overall height of a background planting should not be less than a fifth of the width of the space it surrounds and in any case should not be less than six feet.

The proportions of the garden also need consideration and can be manipu-

Plants can be used, as
in this picture, to
create a sense of space
rather than crowding

lated by positioning of plant groups. A garden in which the length is similar to or less than the width appears squat and static; if the length is $1\frac{1}{2}$ to $2\frac{1}{2}$ times the width the effect is pleasantly calm and the garden appears to be spacious, well proportioned; when the length exceeds three times the width the effect becomes corridor-like and the observer is not encouraged to stop and ponder. Only by subdividing the garden into spaces in which length and width are more in balance can the character of the garden be improved. It should be emphasized here that the garden in this context relates to the space between the plants and not to the whole garden plot, so the proportions of the garden can be very substantially altered by the way in which plants are grouped.

The proportions of the garden space need bear no relationship to the shape of the plot

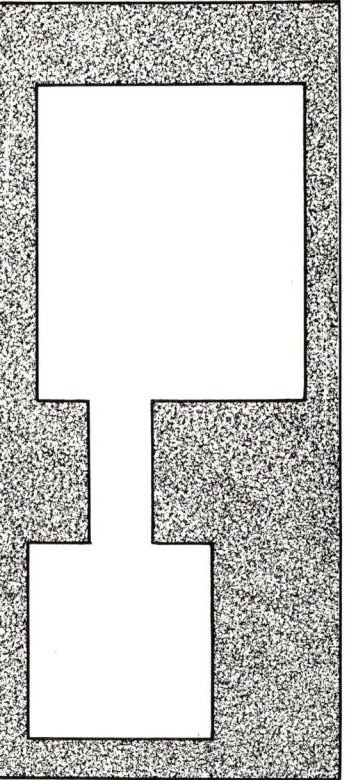

long garden in a square plot

square gardens in a long plot

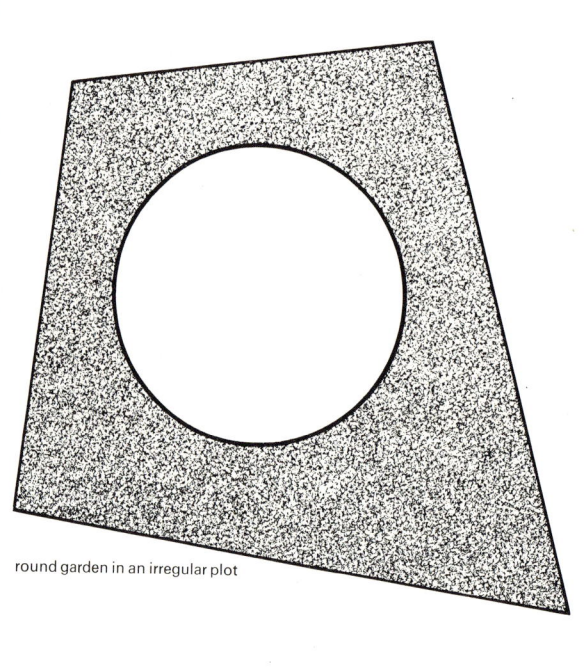

round garden in an irregular plot

30

One important point to emerge from the treatment of the garden as a space rather than as a collection of plants is that the open areas of lawn, paving or water are at least as important in the garden as are the plants. Indeed the easiest way to achieve a satisfying garden layout is to begin by designing the shape of the open area. After all, the lawn is often seen in its entirety whereas only one side of a plant group can be seen from any one point. Too often the separate pieces of a garden – the rose bed, the rockery, the greenhouse, the path – are scattered about the garden leaving a much cut-about lawn with no real sense of enclosure instead of designing the lawn as an attractively shaped sweep and then using plants, rocks, glasshouses and so on to surround and reinforce the shape.

Implicit in this treatment of a garden as a space, an outside room rather than as an area for cultivating plants, is the idea that one is designing *a* garden and all the subordinate parts should contribute to this one composition. Frequently each part is designed as an end in itself: a beautiful rose bed, a magnificent rockery, a splendid pool, a colourful terrace, a decorative wall, and the result is visual chaos. One can imagine the result of an orchestra in which each instrument vied with its neighbours for attention, or a room in which the carpet, the chairs, the curtains, the walls each had distinct characters or an outfit in which the individuality of socks, trousers, shirt and tie were vigorously expressed. In music, in interior design,

in dress we seem to acquire instinctive restraint; in gardens this restraint is too often lacking and the garden suffers from a lack of neutral paving or neutral background planting. Only the calming influence of a lawn has saved many gardens from being complete disasters and only the reduction of the lawn to miniscule proportions in tiny modern gardens has prompted garden owners to find alternative and more satisfactory solutions for their garden designs.

Thus, in considering plants and gardens we need to recognise that the garden is more than a collection of plants; it is a well proportioned open space defined and enclosed by massed plants. The concentrated effect of the garden can be emphasized by neutrality of the background structural planting with limited use of focal points of strong colour or contrasting texture or form.

The use of plants in broad masses has, incidentally, many other advantages. For the plantsman it allows a great many plants to be grown in a very small space, especially if one grows bulbs underneath herbaceous plants underneath shrubs, and for all garden owners it represents a saving of unnecessary effort. The simple outlines of the garden reduce to a minimum the edging and trimming required, and the close growing of plants suppresses weed growth. Although one usually talks of 'cultivating plants' most garden care consists of cultivating the bare ground between the plants and to maintain a continuous cover of plants not only emphasizes the form of the garden but reduces the weeding required. It is imperative, however, before embarking on dense planting and widespread use of ground cover plants, to ensure that the garden is quite free of perennial weeds such as convolvulus (bindweed), ground elder, thistle and couch grass, and to be prepared for a year of hard weeding after planting.

Dense plants smother weed growth by preventing light reaching the soil and by forcing such weed seedlings as do germinate to grow through a thick canopy of leaves and exhaust the food reserves stored in the seed before reaching the light. Ground cover planting is especially effective, therefore, at preventing the growth of small-seeded weeds, the most numerous invaders in most gardens. Perennial weeds have a virtually inexhaustible food supply with which to mount an invasion as they are freely supplied with reserves from the parent plant often growing some feet away. Once the offspring have gained foothold in ground cover they are virtually impossible to remove so every precaution must be taken to eradicate any that exist. It is wise to spend a year removing the perennial weeds if they are especially troublesome, digging deeply to break up the rhizomes and stimulate the fragments into growth. During the summer the new growths are easily removed by forking in the loosened soil, or they can be treated with the appropriate weedkillers. The resourceful gardener can make good use of the year thus spent by growing annuals of similar height and shape to

Annuals are useful for quick effect. The same border photographed in June (left) and September (right)

the intended permanent planting. The castor oil plant (*Ricinus communis*), *Eucalyptus gunnii*, the orange flowered *Tithonia rotundifolia* and giant sunflowers *Helianthus* will frequently soar two or three metres (6 to 10 ft) in one season; *Cosmos*, *Cleome* and *Lavatera* make good middle ground planting of a metre or so (3 to 4 ft) and lower annuals are legion so it is quite possible to simulate the general appearance of a permanent planting scheme with annuals and to see something of the effect in one short season instead of five or ten years. Meanwhile the perennial weeds can be watched for among the annuals as they are sown, planted or staked and can be removed with much less disturbance than is possible among much-branched permanent plants. A final clearance of the annuals in early autumn leaves just enough time for any remaining weed to appear and be disposed of before the winter.

Hand weeding is necessary in the

first year after planting because the disturbance of the soil during cultivation and planting bring to the surface thousands of weed seeds which rapidly germinate and smother the new planting before it has a chance to become established. The hoe can be a lethal weapon amongst trailing ground covers and is reserved for the larger spaces between plants. Once the first crop of weeds is removed – the groundsel, speedwells, chickweed and so on – the other weed seeds germinate only sporadically and the task of weeding becomes much lighter but still important. If one is using the ground cover plants in the usual sense of the word, with plants like periwinkle *Vinca minor* or spotted dead-nettle *Lamium maculatum* in large areas specifically to smother weeds, the initial period of weeding can be quite difficult because weeds and plants become inextricably tangled. The technique to use is to hold the top of the weed with one hand (the left, for a

right-handed person), run the other hand down the stem to the ground and with a firm sustained pull rather than with a sharp tug remove the offending weed by the roots. If a wider range of garden plants is being used as ground cover by close planting, the majority of the plants will have a generally hummocky growth with branches spreading along the ground and perhaps rooting in time. *Geraniums Pelargonium*, *Santolina*, *Epimedium* and many low *Campanula* species have this habit. With such plants the technique is to advance on the weeds from below, gently lifting the skirt of the *Campanula* or whatever with one hand and running the other hand along the surface of the earth, tweaking out the thin stems of weeds and leaving – as often as possible – the stouter grouped stems of the desired plants. Such techniques require a humble posture, bent double with head between the knees if you can manage it, or kneeling and crouching if you cannot. If the latter course is adopted it is a wise precaution to scatter stepping stones at intervals through the area to be covered by plants as they grow, not sufficiently thickly to be able to step casually from one to the other, but enough to be able to hop from one to the other, to gently push aside the neighbouring plants and thus to prepare a kneeling site from which to penetrate the surrounding area. If this is not done one tends to take the line of least resistance through the plants and unwittingly to bulldoze a badger-like trail which never quite closes before the next weeding. All this may make weeding sound like an exercise suitable only for penitent monks but although a delicate operation it is by no means arduous and one has the encouragement that it is excellent for the waistline, and, incidentally, for the temper. The sharp snatches of a bad-tempered gardener are totally ineffective in weeding, the weeds will reappear in much-branched luxuriance, so one is quickly persuaded to a slower and gentler frame of mind appreciated by the family if not by the weeds. Weeding is also an excuse to study the beauties of foliage and flower at close range and many gardeners seem to continue the 'preliminary' weeding long after it is really necessary, searching for the odd struggling groundsel here and there I am sure as an excuse to admire their choice of plants at closer range. Such, however, may not be everyone's idea of delight, and many will be encouraged to hear that, after the first major onslaught and periodic lighter forays in succeeding months, most of the weeds capable of growing will have grown and weeding is reduced to removing the odd intruder before it goes to seed. The exception is with large seeded plants and in most established plantings the main weeds will be oak, sycamore, horse-chestnut and so on, depending on the surrounding trees, but one has the advantage of being able to remove these at leisure.

Chapter 5

Plants and Character

IN CHAPTER 2 the importance of character in gardens was emphasised. Much of that character is determined by the scale, proportion and shape of the space but the same character needs to be carried through in the choice of plants. Thus one might wish to create a lush jungle of a garden, a woodland scene, an elegant architectural composition or a more traditional garden with shrubs and bright flowers around an expanse of smooth, green lawn.

People differ in their opinions of what constitutes a pleasing garden, formal or informal, scrupulously neat or with a casually abandoned appearance, but most would agree on the beauty of natural scenery so it is useful to see how this beauty is achieved and how such knowledge can be put to use in the small garden.

The main characteristic is the great simplicity of plants. Often a few species will dominate several miles of countryside and the beauty is derived not from individual plants but from the contrast between open areas and planting, forest and glade, downland and woodland

Opposite:
A fine example of spires and rounded forms in an herbaceous border

Cat meets dog. Topiary can lift a garden out of the ordinary if used with discretion

clumps or a patchwork of fields with trees marking the hedgerows. Only in scrubland is there a general mixing of trees and open space with no clear dominance of the one or the other, and few people find scrub visually pleasing. Secondly, plants are shaped by the environment in which they grow and in any natural scene, with environmental conditions more or less uniform, even different plants will exhibit generally similar responses. In woodland for example low light intensities, high humidity and shelter from wind cause plants to develop large, thin, pale green leaves and emphasize horizontal branching patterns to trap most of the light available. It is the delicacy of form which appeals in these areas rather than any individual plant. In open, sunny and windy areas plants are more compact with smaller and thicker leaves. In regions of low rainfall the plants may be further protected with grey waxy or hairy coverings to reflect the light and conserve water. Any plants which grow above the wind-shaped carpet of the general vegetation are sparse in leaf and often strikingly shaped by the wind. In gardens, too, it is possible to capture some of this natural beauty by emphasising the distinction between open and planted areas and by choosing plants which are appropriate to each other and to the general theme. Too much emphasis is usually given to contrast in garden literature and in gardens. There is ample choice of material without bringing discordant notes into the garden. In the wild state plants exist in

In natural scenery a single species may dominate miles of countryside

strictly limited areas because they need to survive not only in the particular soil and environment but also in competition with other individuals and species. In gardens geographical barriers to migration are removed and plants are protected from each other and from the severe manifestations of environmental extremes – pests and disease outbreaks, drought or flood. The danger is that the choice becomes too wide; with care one *can* grow succulents and ferns as neighbours but they are not good neighbours.

There are other considerations in the choice of plants. Large-leaved plants tend to overpower small gardens, for example, whereas plants with light-coloured small leaves can give the impression of added space – but such tricks of false perspective are easily overdone. A garden entirely of small-leaved plants lacks excitement just as a small room entirely in white becomes clinical instead of spacious. It is much more satisfactory to make the most of the existing garden's character, to deepen the shade of a shady garden, to use the length of a long narrow garden and to emphasize the intimacy of a small garden rather than trying always to camouflage reality in an attempt to create an impression that the garden is ordinary. Variety is the spice of life: it would be dull indeed if the ladies of the world with their armoury of flat and high-heeled shoes, hair rinses, slimming charts or weight-gaining diets all managed to exactly resemble the Venus de Milo. The same holds true for our gardens.

Bold foliage can be used to create exotic effects: (above) *Gunnera manicata*, (below) *Rheum palmatum*

More bold foliage plants: (above) *Rodgersia tabularis*,
(below) *Lysichitum camtshatsense*

In each garden, then, the character will be determined by the spatial quality and reinforced by the choice of plants and other materials. For a lush jungle of a garden the spaces would be small in scale with little opportunity to escape sufficiently from the planting to view it from a distance. Emphasis would be on large-leaved plants but not always on those of bold form for it is important that the plants merge one into another. For overhead canopy *Catalpa*, *Ailanthus* or the larger leaved climbers (*Vitis coignetiae*, *Actinidia chinensis*) on trellis might be used with the huge umbrellas of *Gunnera manicata* if space permitted. At the lower level *Hosta*, *Rodgersia*, *Rheum* and *Lysichitum* species would clothe the ground with some larger leaved shrubs such as *Fatsia japonica*, *Aralia chinensis*, *Viburnum cinnamomifolium* or where the situation is suitable the larger leaved *Magnolia tripetala* or *Rhododendron* species (R. *falconeri*, R. *fictolacteum*, R. *sinogrande* etc.) to prevent the scene disintegrating with the first frosts. In sheltered areas even the hardy palm *Trachycarpus fortunei* might be used for its exotic appearance. Smooth lawns or expanses of concrete would be inappropriate but paving might be of rough stone, or dark brick or perhaps narrow-joined asphalt blocks. As a less expensive surface, random concrete slabs might be used with creeping thymes *Thymus* or helxine *Soleirolia* in the joints. Flat areas not needed for sitting or walking could be covered with the bright green hummocks of *Festuca eskia*, the darker green *Vinca*

minor or *Hedera* 'Green Ripple'. To contrast with the larger leaves such grassy leaved subjects as *Iris sibirica*, the evergreen *I. foetidissima*, *Liriope*, *Ophiopogon*, the bamboos (especially *Sinarundinaria nitida*) and the grasses themselves (*Stipa gigantea*, *Miscanthus sacchariflorus*, *Pennisetum alopecuroides*) could be used at strategic points. Some of the sedges also possess the necessary qualities but are too invasive for small gardens.

For a woodland character the same spatial quality would be required, small open glades with winding paths through the trees, but the planting would be quite different. For trees and shrubs emphasis would be on species with slender twigs, small buds and small leaves of not too brilliant a colour

or sheen. Birch would be ideal were it not for its dense surface roots. *Amelanchier*, the smaller maples *Acer*, hawthorns *Crataegus*, *Cercidiphyllum*, and hazel *Corylus* are excellent with *Aronia*, *Acer palmatum*, *Corylopsis pauciflora*, *Disanthus* etc. to fill in the shrub layer when necessary. Beneath the trees low plants (primrose *Primula vulgaris*, wood anemone *Anemone nemorosa* and violets *Viola* are superior to many exotic introductions) would be spread in drifts. Care is required in such gardens not to obscure the trunks but to obstruct the view. The calm elegance of woodland is due in large part to the oft-repeated vertical lines of the trunks and to clutter this feature is to destroy the effect, but in small gardens one so easily sees through the trunks to the

The bold foliage and flowers of bear's breeches goes well with the architecture of an older-style house

neighbour's shed or runner beans as some density of planting on the margin becomes essential. This is where the dense twiggery of the aronias, the taller mass of hawthorn and the strategic placing of the occasional evergreen, Portugal laurel *Prunus lusitanica* for example, can be immensely valuable. Where space permits of larger glades, the beautiful dogwoods *Cornus* come into their own. *Cornus florida* (even if it seldom flowers well in Britain) the taller *C. nuttallii* and the smaller but beautifully horizontal *C. controversa* have an elegance of form and a beauty of 'flower' (strictly speaking an inflorescence) unmatched in other plants. *Cornus controversa* lacks the decorative bracts of the others but more than compensates for this in its elegance. Mown grass is appropriate for clearings and elsewhere such low evergreens as *Helleborus foetidus*, *H. argutifolius*, *H. lividus* subsp. *corsicus Pachysandra terminalis* (always an unpleasant yellow-green in the open) and *Vinca minor* can be used to provide some solidity in the ground planting. Paving and other materials should be rough textured but the hand of man need not be entirely banished. Brick, textured concrete, stone (of course) and wood, including the solidity of dark stained railway sleepers, are entirely suitable.

In a modern architectural garden much of the structure is achieved by walls, trellis, fences of sophisticated materials, tubular steel, planed timber and carefully finished concrete, and the function of plants is to provide strong natural forms and relief from the glare faces. *Yucca*, *Fatsia*, *Acanthus*, and *Macleaya* are excellent together with a finer textured loose plant such as

Lamium maculatum, *Festuca glauca* or *Acaena buchananii* and restrained use of climbers – *Clematis viticella* perhaps or *Parthenocissus henryana*.

It would be possible to continue indefinitely with sketch plans for gardens of different characters and the plants to make them but such is not the purpose of this book. I hope, though, that sufficient examples have been given to explain what is meant by character. The idea is similar to the choosing of materials and colours for interior design or for choosing clothes, but while we learn from an early age that pin-stripe suits and brogues, or tweeds and black patent shoes simply do not 'go', the idea of compatibility of plants and other materials is not so widely understood.

The strikingly prickly primate foliage of *Mahonia lomariifolia* reveals its full beauty among low shrubs or a backdrop of ultra-modern architecture

Plants with bold foliage often contrast well with modern architecture: here the bold leaves of *Fatsia japonica* are seen at their best

43

Chapter 6

Plant Grouping

SELECTION of specific plants is dealt with in much greater detail in later chapters but, having discussed the design of gardens in general and the choice of plants to create gardens of character this is an appropriate moment to introduce some general points on the grouping of plants. There are two extremes in grouping: using a large number of plants of one species on the one hand and using one plant each of a great variety of species on the other. Usually in books one sees an intermediate approach recommended, that is to use groups of plants, perhaps three of each in small gardens and seven or more for large gardens. Each of these methods has its advantages.

Using a single species in a garden is rarely possible but one of the most pleasant small gardens I have seen was planted entirely with *Spiraea* x *vanhouttei*. A small circle of lawn was enclosed by the house and garage on two sides and by *Spiraea* on the other two. It was, as a result, well enclosed with a thin film of fresh green in spring, rapidly followed by cascades of white flowers before the new growth took on a pleasant blue-green colour all summer long. *Spiraea vanhouttei* has just a suggestion of autumn colour, reds and browns, then the leaves fall to reveal the warm brown of new growth in winter. It is not a spectacular plant except in its brief period of flower and in mixed plantings it very often looks nondescript and bedraggled but in this small front garden, left to grow as it would, it was dense enough to give privacy even in winter, not so tall as to be overpowering and its subtle changes reflected admirably the changing atmosphere of the different seasons. This is the advantage of very simple planting schemes: in its own small way the garden had much of the form, simplicity and seasonal quality of a miniature beechwood.

Usually one species cannot do everything, providing ground cover, enclosure, overhead canopy and interest of form and colour but I have seen very pleasant gardens relying mainly on a single species, weeping *Forsythia* (*F. suspensa* – so much better than the brilliant yellow *F. x intermedia* 'Specta-bilis') in one case and English yew *Taxus baccata* in another. The *Forsythia* was underplanted with bulbs, violets and bloodroot *Sanguinaria canadensis* for additional interest early in the year and the interest in the yew garden was achieved by beautiful trimming with buttresses, finials and of course the con-trast of smooth lawns. For use as a sole or main planting tall shrubs of rounded form would be required, evergreen or if deciduous then sufficiently dense to provide a reasonable screen. The choke cherry (*Aronia arbutifolia*) with its white flowers, red fruits and brilliant autumn colour would be one obvious plant, *Buddleja alternifolia* a taller but less colourful choice and *Cornus alba* in its various forms another. If time were not important the list could be length-ened by the addition of the strawberry tree *Arbutus unedo* (an evergreen) which is equally attractive as a rounded shrub or tall tree and of *Euonymus alatus*, one of the best shrubs for year-round attractiveness but not a fast grower. One problem with too heavy a reliance on one plant is the susceptibility of the garden to pests and diseases. Most members of the family *Rosaceae*, for example, (cotoneasters, hawthorns, apples, pears, etc.) are susceptible to fire blight and a bad attack could destroy a garden relying heavily on cotoneaster or crab apples for interest.

Although gardens with very simple planting schemes can be immensely satisfying they would not satisfy the readers of gardening books for the simple reason that most gardeners are inveterate plant collectors. In the *For-sythia* garden mentioned earlier, the addition of bulbs and low herbs did not impair the garden's structure or simpli-city and had I had a hand in the garden I should soon have a small tree for height, perhaps something substantial for autumn colour and certainly some low shrubs or herbaceous plants to soften the transition from vertical to horizontal but I should be loath to lose the continuous background of *Forsy-thia*.

The other extreme, the use of a great range of species, has more immediate appeal and is often very suitable for small gardens. In such a mixture no one plant stands out so the effect from any distance is scarcely more varied than the single-species planting but when viewed at close range – and in many modern gardens there is no option *but* to view at close range – there is always something happening: flowers appear here and there and new compositions of foliage are created as plants advance or recede. As well as being of greater botanical interest such plantings also involve more work. Some plants are invariably more vigorous than others and need to be restrained. The restraint of vigorous, the cossetting of slower, plants, and the occasional division of some plants all need to be done with care since the culture of one plant surrounded by many different plants is often not convenient. The gaps left by such operations are not conspicuous and for many owners of small gardens the additional work, never of a really arduous nature, is an advantage rather than a burden. With very mixed plantings the fascinating progress of the seasons is not emphasized. Apart from an increased surge of growth in spring and the catastrophe wrought by the first autumn frosts the garden remains largely unchanged throughout the year but has, nevertheless, a pleasantly furnished appearance. Such schemes are especially useful in creating a casual and luxuriant cottage garden effect in a small space.

In larger gardens, where the main part of the garden is much in excess of two hundred square metres (about 200 square yards) these very fine-textured plantings with 'one of everything' lose their charm. The size of the garden becomes such that, whilst some plants are viewed at close range, most of them are viewed at any one time from a distance and the casual informality becomes an unpleasant jumble: the garden looks untidy and neglected even if there is not a weed to be found. The larger garden needs to be organised into interesting foreground and simple background from the major points of view.

In these larger gardens a good approach is to group the plants so that any one group is easily identified at the greatest distance from which it is to be viewed. Such groups should not be of equal numbers of plants nor of equal size and, odd though it may seem, planting schemes are very much better when the less conspicuous plants are in broad masses with more striking plants

in the minority. The less conspicuous plants are usually less conspicuous because of soft colouring (pale pink, mauve, cream, pale blue), diffuse habit or, very often, because they produce a scattering of flowers over a long period. If relegated to small groups they would tend to be overlooked entirely, whereas if used in broad masses their sparse flowers provide a significant contribution over a long period. Conspicuous plants may be brilliantly coloured (orange, scarlet, chrome yellow, bright blue) or have strong form (large glossy leaves, flowers in spikes) or both. If used in large groups they lose their individuality of form and overshadow more subtle groups. With the correct emphasis in grouping, the less conspicuous plants used in large drifts provide a suitably simple background against which small clumps of more striking plants can be displayed as focal points.

Having sorted out the chorus from the prima donnas, the choice then needs to be made between a diffuse or a concentrated display throughout the year and throughout the garden.

In a large garden there is much to be said for subdividing into smaller compartments for different seasons and Christopher Lloyd, for example, wisely recommends restricting the choice of plants for the main border to those which flower in the summer months. For smaller gardens, however, such an approach is not possible and attempts must be made to have the longest season of interest that can be contrived in the

Dominant plants are set off by broader masses of less conspicuous plants

available space. This is, of course, one of the main objectives of this book and is dealt with specifically in Part IV.

The method of arranging plants throughout the garden again depends on the size of the garden. When gardens are very small and there is little choice but to look *at* the plants it is advisable to have flowers evenly scattered through the garden at all seasons and special attention should of course be given to the selection of plants which are attractive when not in flower. In larger gardens where there is opportunity to look *along* the planting and one would not see all the plants at close hand simultaneously, a better effect is obtained by grouping together plants which are to flower at the same time. In this way, all the plants flowering at a particular time will support each other in visual effect to form a focal point against a general green background of other plants which have finished or have yet to flower. If plants in large gardens are dispersed, there is not enough colour to be appreciated from a distance and at close range the appeal of flowers is lessened by surrounding plants which have finished flowering and are in a more or less advanced state of senescence. In neither instance can the plants be fully appreciated.

It is possible to increase the colourfulness of planting schemes very substantially by interplanting very early and very late subjects so that each lives a more or less separate existence in the same piece of ground. This is dealt with fully in Part IV. Even greater improvement can be had by moving plants into a border for their flowering season and replacing them when finished. Such operations, intermediate between permanent borders and seasonal bedding, obviously require additional resources in terms of greenhouse, cold frame or at least nursery space and may be beyond the scope of most people with very small gardens. Some ideas are given, however, in Chapter 16. Each of these elaborations comes nearer to the situation in which the whole garden is colourful all year long but it is important to consider whether or not such a goal should ever be achieved. One of the most valuable attributes of the garden is change, and one reason that very simple plantings are so successful is that the change is most marked. A constant riot of colour would soon be taken for granted and provide no pleasure whatsoever. Surely the most damning criticism of plastic plants (by which means we could achieve permanently colourful gardens) is not that they are fake, nor crude – but that they do not change.

Thus we can find consolation in the fact that our gardens are not perfect all the time for only with these shortcomings can we fully appreciate the brief but increasingly frequent moments when it nears perfection.

Chapter 7

Plants and Work

The pet/child/
weed-proof qualities
of a garden depend
on the plants used in it

LABOUR saving is a relative term when applied to gardens. Most plants grow and require eventual restraint. Those which fail to grow need replacement. None stand still. Only the petrol-station gardens of concrete, pebbles and plastic conifers are entirely labour-free and even most of these would benefit from an occasional dusting. Writers who proclaim that, with a scattering of ground cover plants, a shrubbery or two and a sprinkle of weedkiller, acres of garden will look after itself are to be regarded with the gravest suspicion. It is true to say, though, that plants and groupings vary enormously in the attention they require and that one can choose to a very considerable degree the amount and type of work which the garden will generate by suitable choice and arrangement of plants and other materials. It is also true to say (although often forgotten in the mass of labour-saving literature) that gardeners vary enormously in the amount and type of effort they wish to give. Indeed it is one of the ironies of a gardener's life that he starts

49

his working life too poor to afford a large garden and has to keep himself busy in a tiny patch; in middle age he is too busy earning his fortune to keep up the garden he can now afford and when at last retirement brings both time and resources his energy is spent. Most of us, then, begin life with a flurry of alpines, annuals and herbaceous perennials and soon begin the long process of 'grassing down' and 'shrubbing up' before finally bowing out.

The simplest gardens to maintain are those with large areas of paving or grass. The former can be expensive, of course, and the latter requires the constant attention of mowing and, in most instances, weeding, feeding, pest and disease control, but all of these operations can be mechanised and some people enjoy machines and gadgetry as much as gardens. Mechanically minded or not, there is much to be said for broad expanses of grass but be sure that they are broad expanses for a large lawn takes very little more time to manage than a small one and a lawn cluttered with posts, paths, flower beds and trees not only looks cluttered but necessitates hours of edging, trimming and snipping in corners inaccessible to the mower.

Shrubs are reputed to be labour saving and to a considerable extent this is so. Certainly the ground needs to be prepared for planting only once (incidentally, preparation should therefore be as thorough as possible) and few shrubs require staking or regular division. There are, however, limitations in the use of shrubs alone. Firstly they are expensive although this is not always terribly important as they may cover more ground than less expensive herbaceous plants and are, in any case, to be regarded as long term investments. Mainly, however, shrubs are slow to reach their ultimate size. This means that shrub gardens are very thin in their early years and often too crowded in later years. Moreover, the better, more permanent plants are the slower growing ones and one is faced either with a long wait for the garden to reach maturity or with the cost of a quick effect both in financial terms and in the constant attacks with the pruning saw necessary to keep the garden under control in subsequent years.

Except in small, walled gardens however shrubs must form a major part of the backbone of the garden and the problems inherent in their slow growth are overcome by using fillers or by initial generous planting. When shrubs are mixed with herbaceous and other plants then much of the initial height and bulk can be created with herbaceous plants, allowing the shrubs to grow on in their own good time to add solidity to the scheme.

One great advantage of considering the garden as a spatial design is that much of the effect is achieved as soon as the ground plan is marked out and the plants have achieved a height of two metres (6 ft) or so, whereas in gardens relying on maturity of individual specimens for effect the wait is measured in decades. As one is relying

on general plant form rather than the particular species, it is possible to use very quick growing plants among the permanent planting and to thin them out as the permanent inhabitants fill their allotted area.

The brooms are ideal fillers for use in this way. Spanish broom (*Spartium junceum*) for example grows quickly from seed to form sizeable plants in three years. Brooms are not long lived plants in most cases and will often remove themselves without being asked as neighbouring plants grow. They do not form new shoots readily from the base and so can be sawn off at ground level when no longer wanted, leaving the nitrogen-fixing nodules with which they are blessed to enrich the soil. As if

these were not advantages enough, Spanish broom will also flower for most of the summer, a very bright yellow and beautifully scented. Second on the list of temporary fillers is *Buddleja davidii*. It is a popular shrub and easily grown from hardwood cuttings so if one has friends with gardens it is usually unnecessary to stoop to buying plants. It grows even taller than Spanish broom but is less dense. The flowers, in spikes of rich red or purple are beloved of butterflies and appear in late summer when most shrubs have been long forgotten. I am never quite sure whether I prefer the *Buddleja* cut to the ground annually to produce astonishingly long shoots with enormous spikes of flower but with a winter silhouette which makes a worn-

Shrubs and herbaceous plants together result in rapid establishment, more effective cover and a longer season of interest

Opposite:
An established
mixture of shrubs and
herbaceous plants in
a four year old
garden

Opposite below:
*Paeonia
mlokoszewitschii*, a
beautiful but fleeting
flower with
long-lasting foliage

out besom broom look attractive, or left to grow into quite a pleasant small tree with hundreds of smaller spikes – and even more hundreds of butterflies – but with its freely displayed inheritance of previous years' dead flowers and branches marring the scene. One advantage of growing it as a filler for five years or so is that there is neither time nor necessity to decide. *Escallonia*, *Forsythia*, the larger *Spiraea* species and *Leycesteria formosa* are other satisfactory fillers but suffer, approximately in the order listed, of being too bulky for the well-being of the plants that are to follow. Whereas broom retreats before other advancing vegetation and *Buddleja* leaps skyward with no thought of malice towards its slower brethren, *Escallonia* and the others mentioned above insist on throwing vigorous and dense branches into and around the permanent plants, discouraging their already hesitating steps towards maturity. Although not tall enough to qualify as background planting mention must be made of *Ceanothus* 'Gloire de Versailles' as a shrub which is ideal for rapidly filling the middle ground. It seems to grow admirably on our chalk, on heavy yellow clay and beneath the shade of old flowering cherry trees so it cannot be described as difficult. As it is one of the obliging plants like *Buddleja*, which can be cut almost to the ground, it can be allowed to advance at will then forced to retreat before the secateurs until it is removed if, indeed, removal is the fate finally decreed.

Group planting is useful when lower shrubs – heathers, *Hebe*, *Cistus* – are to be used. As a group of trees or shrubs eventually takes the form of a single mature specimen and as small plants move more successfully and grow more quickly than large ones it is better to buy several small plants and to space them close together in an area which would normally be covered by one much larger plant. The cost of plants rises very steeply with size so one can often get ten young plants for the cost of one larger one. Buying five, therefore, saves money as well as hastening the garden's development.

Almost all shrubs reduce work by avoiding the need for regular replanting but many are even more useful in preventing weed growth by covering the soil. Enormous lists of ground cover shrubs could be made but heathers (*Calluna*, *Erica*, *Daboecia*), horizontal conifers, *Cistus*, *Hebe* and *Berberis* are among the most useful. They only suppress weeds of course, in proportion to the degree in which they shade the soil. Such tall open growers as lilacs, *Philadelphus* and *Buddleja davidii* are quite ineffective at reducing weed growth. Whilst one turns automatically to shrubs for permanence and solidity, many herbaceous plants are much more effective, and even more important, much quicker ground covers, but their use for this purpose is considered fully in Chapter 15.

One final comment on shrubs at this stage, on pruning. My usual advice on pruning is 'don't'. It is sometimes necessary to drastically reduce the size

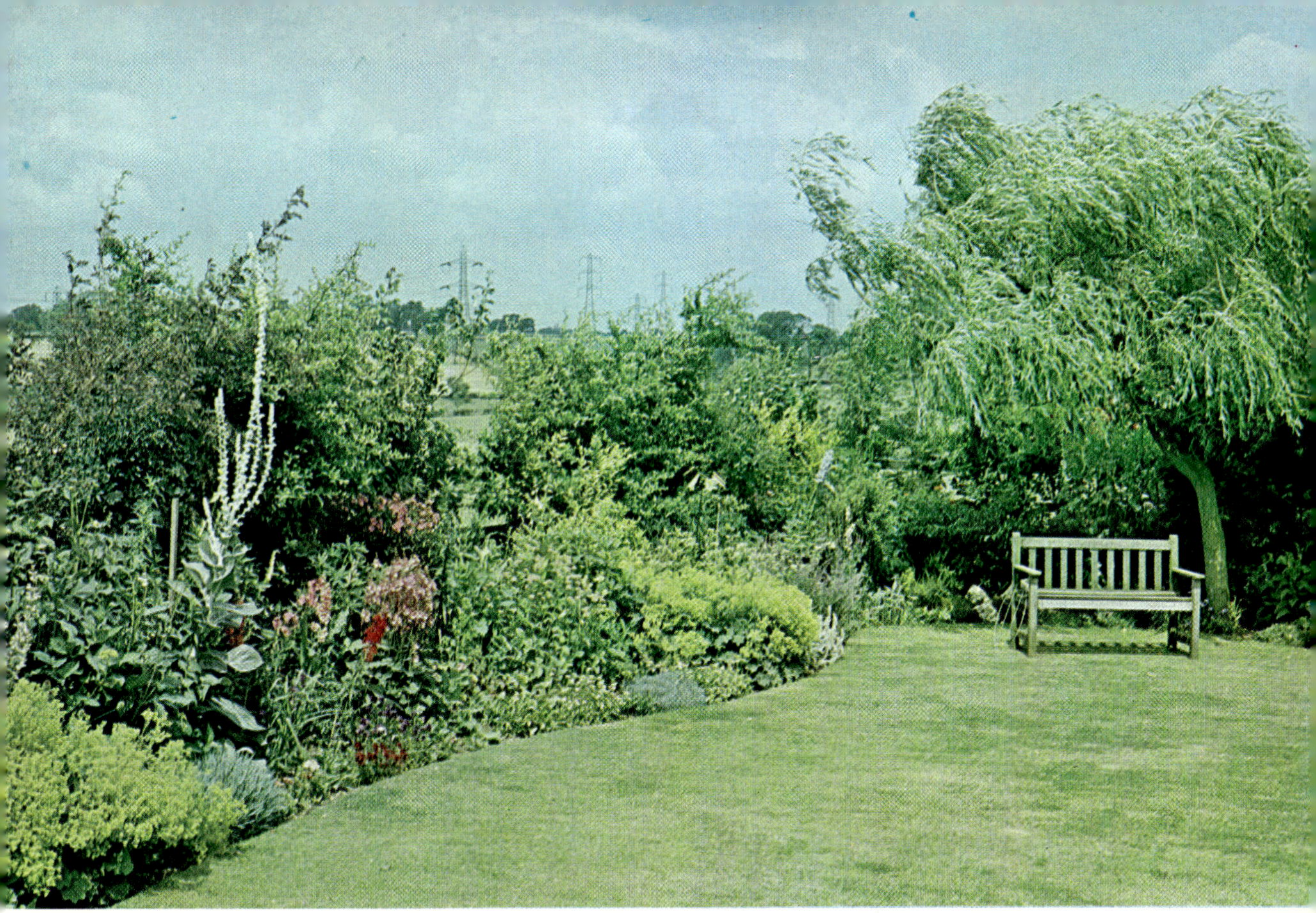

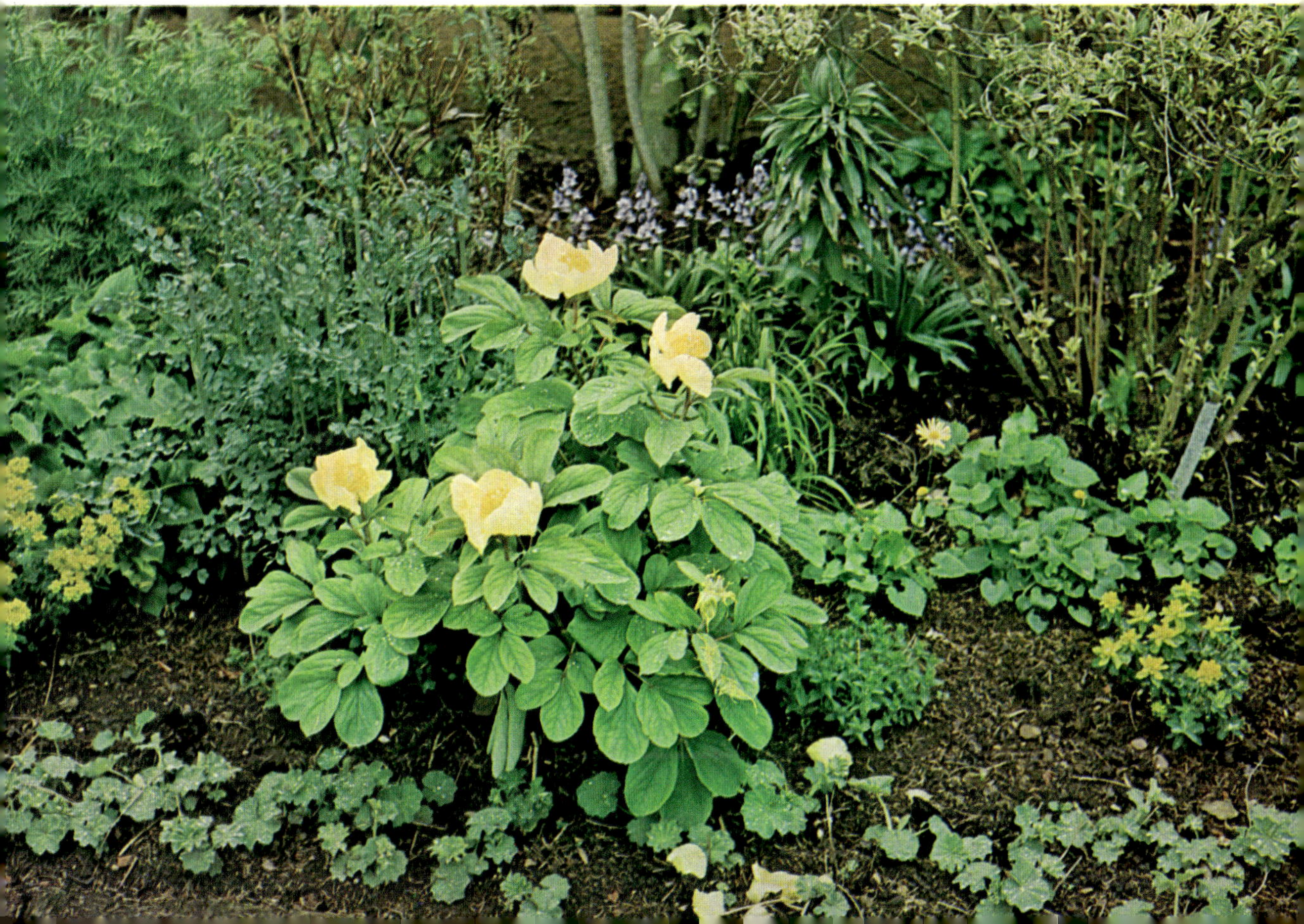

of a shrub and give it a new lease of life but annual mutilations to keep a plant in bounds signify the wrong choice of plant. For years I followed exhortations to remove spent growth after flowering or cut hard back in the early spring but have gradually realised that plants left to their own devices have a marvellous ability to grow into graceful spreading domes so I have gradually forsaken the handful of magnificent flowers on a few sparse stems in favour of nature's bounty.

Shrubs, then, appeal because of their permanence, the height which they contribute to the garden and their labour-saving properties, whereas herbaceous plants are currently out of favour, conjuring up visions of mammoth lifting, dividing and replanting operations,

Opposite:
A tiny vegetable garden exhibited by the 'Financial Times' at Chelsea

Opposite below:
Runner beans (on pole) lend themselves to the flower garden

Philadephus badly pruned reveals its full horror in winter – such ugliness for little gain in flower-power

Philadelphus left unpruned makes a large relaxed shrub, smothered in flowers

forests of brushwood staking and mountains of debris to be removed to the compost heap or bonfire each autumn. Such visions obscure the great value of many excellent herbaceous plants which require no more care than the majority of shrubs. There are six and two halves which top the list as being of value in most gardens.

Anemone hupensis var. *japonica*, the Japanese anemone, is first alphabetically and in favour. It has excellent fresh green foliage appearing rather late in the spring but providing a good ground covering carpet about 30 cm (1 ft) high. From August onwards the carpet gets taller as the slender stems bear aloft whole forests of flowers – white or pink – light enough to give height at the front of borders and beautiful enough to be used in large drifts wherever an excuse can be found. It seems to tolerate most soils and is long lived even when found in dark neglected corners, under trees and in other places that one would not usually dream of casting beautiful flowers. Far from requiring division it positively shrinks after moving and, growing well from root cuttings, one usually finds it growing much better in the place from which it was moved than in the place to which it was transferred! *Hemerocallis* come close second on the list. Even if they did not tolerate a wide range of soils (they tolerate rather than luxuriate in our few inches of gravel over chalk but continue to increase steadily), grow in sun and shade and form impenetrable clumps of excellent grassy foliage they

would still be grown for their engaging habit of producing their new foliage of a bright and cheery pale green very early in the year, often in February, and long before any other plants are about their business. The flowers are brilliant and although each lasting only a day (hence the common name of 'day lily') are produced in succession over several weeks. The orange and yellow hybrids still seem to me to be the real day lilies. Many of the older 'pink' hybrids were yellow/apricot exaggerations of the catalogue-writers' pen but there are now some excellent pink and true crimson hybrids. Paeonies and *Dictamnus albus* have in their favour longevity and elegant foliage. Having once had to weed some much neglected forty-year-old paeony beds I have a great respect for their persistence in adversity. My favourite has been *P. officinalis*, the old double red paeony. It flowers before the June superabundance of flowers and is low enough to lean rather than collapse onto the ground, for paeonies really should be staked, and the leaves are a respectable green/purple for much of the summer. It must also be more portable than others as one plant was moved three times in twelve months, the last time when the flowers were about to open and it still flowered then and in subsequent years. The paeony is an extravagance among flowers, gorgeous but fleeting, and if paeonies you must have, then visit the nursery in the autumn, select the best foliage and trust in the catalogue description of the flower. They are all beautiful but foliage quality is not so reliable. *Paeonia delavayi* confuses the issue here by being half-shrubby, a tree paeony but as it has excellent leaves, pleasant but not exciting flowers and grows in our garden behind a yew hedge and in the dense rooty shade of a cherry it must have a mention. The most recent arrival is *P. mlokosewitschii* which has ousted *P. officinalis* from favour. It is fleeting even among the paeonies, flowering well only for a day or two, but the flower is beautiful, a pale yellow globe and the foliage excellent. It emerges looking just like forced rhubarb, a delicious watery pink stem with pale green top but unfolds to a pale blue grey round-lobed leaf which stays in excellent condition all summer. Last on the short list are two very different plants. *Ceratostigma plumbaginoides* suffers a worse handicap from plant-naming botanists than does *Paeonia mlokosewitschii* but is a useful late flowering sprawling mat of a plant. Just as the blue flowers appear in September–October the leaves turn plum purple to provide a good background. This plant appears very late in the spring and is ideal for smothering the remains of bulbs. *Aruncus sylvester* has been pushed about by botanists from its former *Spiraea aruncus* but is at least pronounceable. It is a large plant 1.5 m (5 ft) or more tall in flower, forming large spreading clumps of leaves looking like overgrown Japanese anemones, topped in June by feathery plumes of creamy white. These fade but remain decorative for two months or more. Out-

wardly it resembles a large *Astilbe* in every respect save the fact that it grows quite well in surprisingly dry soils so for permanence, tolerance and elegance it is a fitting member of this short list.

The two halves referred to are *Hosta* and *Brunnera*. *Hosta* because I have never associated it with herbaceous borders and therefore do not think of it automatically as herbaceous, which of course it is, and *Brunnera* because, although the emphasis here is on labour saving, our *Brunnera* does receive some fussing. *Hosta* are currently, and justifiably, the most fashionable of plants. They are permanent, they are weed proof in large clumps, they have superb foliage of green, blue, white or yellow in various combinations and many have quite useful flowers: *H. plantaginea* (*H. subcordata*) is a flowering plant in its own right with spikes of scented white flowers in August. *But* they require moist soils to do well, except perhaps *H. lancifolia* which, although good and having good lilac flowers, is not as impressive as its larger brethren, and in moist soils they are subject all too often to the depredations of slugs. *Brunnera macrophylla* (formerly *Anchusa myosotidiflora*) does not require attention, it grows in wet or dry soils, in sun or shade, and its light branching spikes of vivid forget-me-nots are borne above large very un-forget-me-not like leaves before any other herbaceous plants except doronicums are in flower. It looks as though it should be divided regularly, growing higher and higher out of the ground, but never suffers

from being left. Our one extravagance is to remove the dead flower stalks which quite ruin the appearance of the excellent soft green leaves if allowed to remain. It is a slow job: one can snatch off the leafless flower stems at the risk of removing a few of the newly developing crowns, thus hastening the procedure and this is a risk well worth taking, as even when one diligently searches out the base of each flower spike to snip with secateurs there are always occasions when a large new leaf is cut off instead of or with the flower stem.

Bulbs, too, can often be left in the ground at least for several years. *Narcissus*, *Crocus* and most of the small bulbs increase steadily if conditions are suitable and, although one is usually advised to lift tulips every year (a necessary procedure when bedding out), they too can usually be left for several years if the soil is well drained. The newer dwarf hybrids of *Tulipa fosterana*, *T. greigii* and *T. kaufmanniana* will often increase rapidly to form large clumps spectacular in flower. Because of their great value in small gardens, bulbs receive special attention in Chapter 14.

The demanding plants are the transient ones, the non-hardy perennials – *Pelargonium*, *Dahlia*, *Fuschia* – the hardy and half-hardy annuals. These require a nursery area with a greenhouse, preferably heated, for overwintering perennials and propagation facilities in the spring. The sowing, thinning, cultivation and weed control of these young plants are very important and very time consuming operations. Most of the plants, however, are very colourful over a very long period and amply reward any care which is given. Of course the plants can be bought 'ready-made' in May or June for planting directly into the garden or a great deal can be done with improvised facilities in airing cupboards and on window sills but one still needs to plant into cultivated soil each year and weeds are still going to grow and to require removal every year until the plants have spread sufficiently to cover the ground.

Enough should have been said, however, to demonstrate that the choice of plants and their arrangement will determine how much work is necessary in the garden. It is for the gardener, then, to decide which plants to use.

Opposite:
Hosta subcordata, as useful for its late, scented flowers as for its striking foliage

Chapter **8**

The Vegetable Garden

THE emphasis of this book is on ornamental plants and ornament will long continue to be the main function of most small gardens – but it is not the only function. The tremendous increase of interest in home-grown vegetables and fruit in very recent years has been sufficiently remarkable to have excited comment from people in all aspects of horticulture. Whether the interest is due to foreign holidays stimulating a desire for unusual foods unobtainable through normal retail channels or to the increasing discernment with regard to flavour and quality of fresh vegetables or to the necessity of combating in some way the soaring price of food in the shops is a matter of conjecture. All three factors and others here unmentioned probably contribute. It is clear, however, that this is a long-term change and that any book dealing with the general disposition of garden uses must devote some consideration to vegetables and fruit if it is to be of any value. This chapter has therefore been included to offer some suggestions for the incorporation of fruits and vegetables into a small garden in such a way that they are decorative as well as useful.

One unfortunate legacy of the nineteenth century is the belief that beauty and utility must be opposed, hence the frantic attempts to conceal any utilitarian object or to plaster it with surface decoration. In the arts in general we have now returned to a position of appreciating that simple utilitarian design can be beautiful in itself and certainly this belief can be demonstrated very clearly in gardens. It is invariably the bad siting of garden buildings, for example, rather than their appearance as such which causes offence.

The first point to be made about the vegetable garden, then is that it is *not* inherently ugly. However, whilst one can admire the 'functional integrity' of a well-grown Brussels sprout plant, it hardly presents a pleasing sight in the winter when widely spaced in straight ranks in an otherwise informal garden. Even the smell leaves something to be desired! When vegetables and cut-flowers are required in quantity, there-

fore, they are undoubtedly best grown in a separate kitchen-garden where their requirements for a deeply worked fertile soil, full sun and a variety of stakes, cloches, bird nets and other paraphenalia can be attended to without hindrance. Even where such a possibility exists, however, one need not banish the kitchen garden automatically to the furthermost point from the house. Instead it should be used to add to the spatial interest of the garden. In many older gardens, at Road Farm, Churt and at Tintinhull, Somerset for example, the main path of the kitchen garden is flanked by flower borders and espalier fruit so the length of the kitchen garden provides an attractive vista which adds to the sense of expansiveness. In some gardens the fruit was obviously trained with loving care to form arbours, arches and arcades, adding greatly to the delights of the garden. Even in smaller gardens the placing of the kitchen garden in a central position rather than at the end adds to the variety of spaces in the garden.

If your interest in vegetable growing

A border of espalier fruit trees and flowers create an extended vista through the vegetable garden

61

increases and the size of garden shrinks, it is inevitable that a situation is reached when it is no longer possible to have a separate kitchen garden unless one adopts the scheme of mediaeval and early Elizabethan gardens, devoting the whole area to fruits, vegetables and herbs. There is no doubt that such a garden, with expanses of freshly dug soil and neat rows of well-grown plants, would be attractive but the enforced close view of such a garden is not conducive to its full enjoyment. A less radical solution to the problem of limited space would be to limit the selection of utilitarian plants to those which are also attractive.

With fruit this presents no problems. Apples, pears, plums and so on are attractive flowering trees and apples in particular are very amenable to training. Beware, though, the temptation to grow bush forms rather than trees in small gardens. Where a large apple tree can be left largely to its own devices it can provide the focal point of a garden, the height and canopy, leaving room for people and plants to live

Variety of garden spaces created by placing vegetable garden centrally

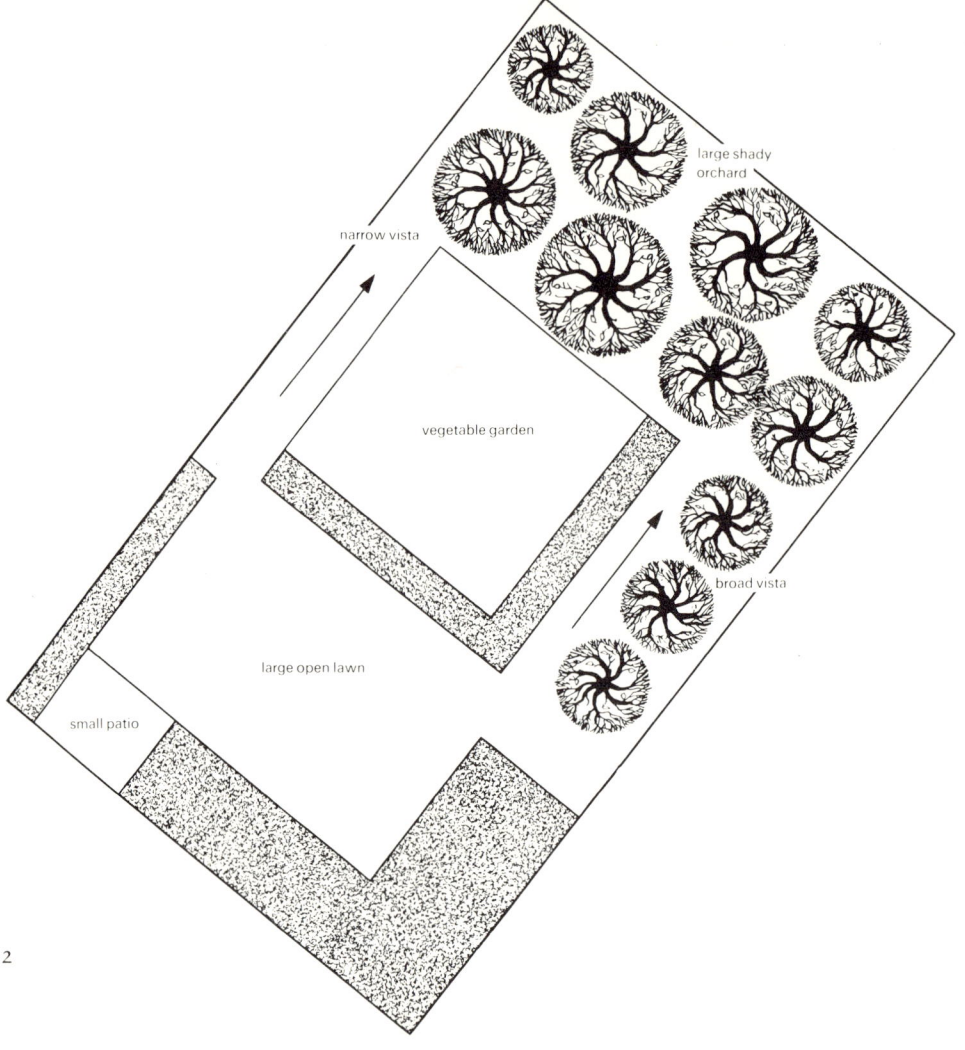

large shady orchard

narrow vista

vegetable garden

broad vista

large open lawn

small patio

beneath its branches. Apples grown as bushes on fairly vigorous rootstocks will expand much nearer to ground level, leaving room only for primroses and the most recumbent gardeners. If there really is no room for a tree then apples can be grown as cordons, espaliers or fans to form useful and beautiful screens or wall decoration, as can the other tree fruits. Blackcurrant foliage often displays attractive autumn colour and even though none of the bush fruits are spectacularly ornamental I see no reason why they should not

provide height and form in a mixed planting with more obviously attractive plants between them. Strawberries make very effective ground cover and I know of one garden in which the non-trailing alpine strawberry forms an attractive carpet over a formal rosebed. The more exotic fruits such as fig, grape, peach or even oranges in tubs are at least as appropriate to the ornamental garden as to the fruit garden and given the care which can often be expended in small gardens plus the shelter which usually prevails, the monetary value of

A well trained fruit tree has a beauty all its own

63

their fruit crop is likely to be far higher than that derived from wall-trained apples.

Even with vegetables the scope is considerable. The grosser brassicas will probably be omitted as will potatoes (although the latter, like the tomato, was long grown as a flowering plant before its culinary value was recognized) because the yields obtained from very small plantings are scarcely worth the room. Personal taste intervenes here as indeed throughout the book: potato foliage is quite attractive and some gardeners might care to plant a few tubers of early potatoes in a large pot to be started indoors and later stood out in a sheltered position for the sake of a very early crop of new potatoes. Others might find ornamental cabbage sufficiently of merit to be included in the garden. There are, however, many plants of more obvious charm.

Runner beans are certainly worthy of consideration as ornamental climbers for the sake of their prolific red flowers and the range is now widened to include white and pink flowered types. Peas have little merit, although they are not especially unsightly, but the asparagus pea *Tetragonolobus purpureus* is a much more attractive trailing plant with

flowers of deep maroon. Be sure, though, to pick the pods while small because they quickly become *very* stringy and the seeds, resembling sweet-pea rather than edible pea are not to be recommended when hard! The tomato, which I suppose should be included as a fruit rather than a vegetable, has not a very colourful flower but it has the interest of other *Solanaceae* (including the potato already mentioned) and of course the fruits are eminently attractive to the eye and the palate. Another plant causing fruit/vegetable arguments is rhubarb. It is a vegetable. It is also a very splendid foliage plant and a stately flowering plant if given the opportunity. Our rhubarb is now sited at the end of the wild garden and I heartily recommend it for any position where the vegetable garden encroaches on the flower garden calling for partial con-Other attractive foliage plants include carrot, curly kale, beetroot (especially the brilliantly red-stemmed chard or sea-kale beet) and parsley. Marrows have bold, attractively silver-mottled foliage and one of the more interesting small gardens on my way to work is planted with one marrow. It completely engulfs the garden each year in a highly attractive manner and effectively controls any

Many vegetables have attractive foliage

weed foolish enough to appear above ground. The effect after frost is ghastly. I wish the owner would invest in at least a few crocus for the pre-marrow season but five or six months of pleasure from one plant plus an indefinite supply of courgettes is not to be scorned. Lettuce was never an ugly plant but the recent development of non-hearting salad-bowl lettuce has raised this salad to the status of an ornamental plant. Indeed, while one wonders at some of the activities of plant breeders, their attempts to tailor many vegetable crops to the small garden are eminently praiseworthy.

Many vegetables, while lacking in beauty are not exactly ugly either. Into this category comes the onion, dwarf French bean, parsnip and so on. The ranks of utilitarian beauty could also be expanded by including the herbs, hyssop, lavender, rosemary, sage and thyme for evergreen interest, chives, fennel, dill, angelica and other less permanent plants for the more adventurous. Indeed the sudden interest in herb gardens has come so quickly that one suspects that many gardeners are growing herbs for their charm alone, with no intention of using any but the most basic in the kitchen.

Enough has been said, I think, to indicate that considerable potential exists for the ornamental use of vegetables but the ways in which they might be used merits some mention.

One way, and perhaps the most generally useful, is to continue to group vegetables into one part of the garden but, by concentrating on small and attractive plants, to obviate the requirement for screening in a garden which is too small for such high divisions. A very interesting small garden was shown at the Chelsea Flower Show some time ago with a little box hedge and a statue forming the background for selected small vegetables and strawberries. It was, in effect, a scaled-down version of the great French potagers or kitchen-gardens such as that at Villandry. There is no reason why such a feature should not occupy a position of some prominence near the house, perhaps extending the usual notion of a herb garden to include carrots, lettuce and other low-growing vegetables. To further enhance the productivity of the little garden the statue might rest elsewhere for the summer to make way for a pillar of runner beans or a tomato plant or the more statuesque rosettes of globe artichoke. A clipped bay tree would also form a logical and more permanent focal point.

The other way of growing vegetables, of which I must confess I have no first hand experience, is to dissolve the barriers completely between ornamental and utilitarian plants. Our garden is sufficiently large to accommodate a separate area for vegetables and cut-flowers but I was delighted to see my theories carried into practice in some Swiss and Austrian chalet gardens with tomatoes, roses, potatoes, begonias and lettuce growing together in great profusion. The vegetable gardener already indulges in catch-cropping and intercropping, techniques very similar to those described for the flowery mead in the major part of this book, so the possibilities for combining flowers and vegetables are endless.

With the exception of rhubarb, globe artichoke and a very few others the vegetables recommended are annuals and most of them can be considered as hardy summer annuals to be sown outside from March or half-hardy annuals to be planted out from late May or June. The difficult vegetables are the early crops to be sown in March and mature in mid-summer, early carrots and lettuce for example but these can be rotated with curly kale, or less ornamentally, leeks. The others, acting much like hardy or half-hardy annuals can follow spring bedding plants in the usual manner. As soil preparation for vegetables is usually thorough it would be unwise to associate permanent spring bulbs with vegetable patches but polyanthus and pansy in particular benefit greatly from generous treatment and could be removed to resting quarters to allow vegetables to be grown.

There are, of course, problems associated with this method of vegetable cultivation. Deep digging and manuring of small patches of garden among permanent plants is not easy and sowing of vegetable seeds in straight rows will often be less attractive than broadcast sowing despite the added weeding problems inherent in broadcasting seed. Taking vegetables as required means that the patches will become thinner and thinner before replanting can be done and, whereas it is possible to lift all the carrots and store them for use, it is not possible to store lettuce for any length of time. Nevertheless if the vegetables form a relatively minor part of the overall planting scheme the additional work will be equally minor, and the gradual loss of plants to the kitchen will not be noticed in the overall profusion of growth if individual patches of vegetables are kept small. The benefits of beauty and utility should greatly outweigh the inconvenience as should the advantages outweigh the disadvantages in any good compromise.

As noted earlier, garden design involves a series of logical compromises, and if the need for vegetables is such that a border is in a continuous state of depopulation and upheaval then this particular combination of beauty and utilitarian format for the garden, perpromise and the gardener would be better advised to adopt a more strictly utilitarian format for the garden perhaps with an edging of flowers and attractively trained fruits along the paths or boundaries. In many situations this extension of a cottage garden idea could prove quite delightful.

Part Three

The Garden
in Winter

TO RETURN to the purely ornamental garden, winter is the best time to begin looking at the garden with a view to potential improvement, for two reasons.

Firstly it is in the winter months that the greatest gains are to be made: even in the least inspiring of gardens there is usually a scattering of flowers to be had in the summer and the general greenery of spreading foliage serves to distract the eye from the garden's imperfections, the sagging fences and cracked paths, whereas in winter the tattered remains of summer's glory serve only to add to the general air of desolation. In most areas to which this book is distributed, winter lasts as long as summer – and it seems to last much longer! It is surprising therefore that the subject of the winter garden is still much neglected despite the appearance

Helleborus multifidus, one of the greenest of green flowers: a gem for the winter garden

Opposite:
The garden in winter

from time to time of several interesting books on the topic. With little trouble the garden can be full of interest throughout the winter and the plants recommended here are not difficult to obtain or to grow.

Secondly, any improvement in the winter aspect of a garden must be counted pure gain. The plants which contribute either disappear completely soon after flowering to leave room for summer display, the case for the many beautiful bulbs, or they remain to add foliage and form to the general greenery of summer. If therefore the garden can be made attractive in winter then it is certain to be at least as satisfactory throughout the seasons.

Small gardens have distinct advantages over their more expansive counterparts when it comes to design for winter as they are usually more sheltered and the general greyness of the winter sky does not intervene to mar the scene as is so often the case in larger gardens. True the owner of a large garden can resort to ideas not available to the small gardener for improving winter gardens, using large groups of coloured stemmed plants for example but he would do well to learn a lesson which is forced upon the small garden owner and group most of the winter flowers in particular, near the house where they can be enjoyed from a sheltered vantage point and where they can remain for the rest of the year as a simple green foreground to more colourful views of the garden.

In all but the smallest gardens winter emphasizes the need for simplicity. Compare, for example, the beauty of a group of birch or a beechwood in winter with the dismal chaos of a jumble of dead and dying plants in our gardens. Rather than trying to disguise winter it is better to enjoy its positive aspects with solid evergreens, delicate tracery of stems and occasional fragile flowers.

Opposite:
Two very different evergreen plantings for winter interest. *Viburnum tinus*, *V. davidii*, *Mahonia japonica* and golden privet create a tall screen with foliage and winter flowers. Yucca, santolina and bergenia create evergreen interest on a lower level

73

Chapter 9

Evergreen Plants

EVERGREEN plants form the backbone of the garden for only in larger gardens are the massed trunks of deciduous trees and shrubs sufficient to provide the necessary degree of enclosure. Too heavy a reliance on evergreens might tend to make the garden sombre and would certainly reduce the main joy of spring, the bursting forth of fresh green buds on leafless plants but the term evergreen covers a multitude of colours and forms so there is ample material from which to choose.

The larger evergreens – yew, holly, laurel – are too big in their fully grown state for most gardens but there are many ways in which they can be used even in small gardens. There are some very good slow-growing yews: *Taxus cuspidata* 'Nana' is densely rounded and can be used either as a very low formal hedge or as a shrub. Annual cutting back of its new growth causes it to assume an irregular hummocky shape like a cumulus cloud and it is sufficiently slow growing to add solidity to the foreground of even the smallest garden for

decades. *Taxus baccata* 'Fastigiata', the upright Irish yew has a habit reminiscent of groves of conifers ranging up a mountain slope and is one of the few vertical plants which could be wholeheartedly recommended as a background. It is, however, a very large plant at maturity and the effect of its dark solid spires is better achieved in small gardens by planting a group of the dwarf *Taxus media* 'Hicks'. Hollies *Ilex* are both large and uncomfortable but in their early years are slow growing and compact and they can be made to keep this compact habit indefinitely by judicious pruning, any long vigorous growths usually being removed just before December 25th. All the evergreen hollies are valuable for their highly polished leaves but the variegated forms such as 'Silver King' and 'Silver Queen' add a cheery note to the winter garden, having none of the sickly, chlorotic appearance of many other variegated plants. We think almost automatically of *Ilex aquifolium* when holly is mentioned but another species, *I. pernyi* is also useful, with lighter green leaves, again highly polished but of a slender shape and borne gracefully on slightly drooping branches. This is a smaller plant than our native holly and will bear berries when only a metre or so (3–4 ft) high. The laurels, both cherry laurel (*Prunus laurocerasus*) and Portugal laurel (*P. lusitanica*) are too big and too shapeless for small gardens but they deserve consideration as small trees of character. If lower branches are removed (rather than encouraged as when using laurel as a hedge) both plants form interesting small trees with irregular trunks and a rounded canopy which is of course evergreen. Both flower freely with white spikes of 'bird-cherry' flowers and the cherry laurel takes on quite an exotic appearance. I prefer, however, the darker, denser and more graceful canopy of Portugal laurel.

Garrya elliptica is a plant to be recommended even as a temporary resident of the smallest garden, flowering as it does even as a small plant. In summer it might euphemistically be described as 'a good foil' because its dull olive green rounded leaves are so unremarkable as to draw attention to themselves. In late summer however the ends of its branches display small green catkins, expanding during the winter to form long drooping tassels of pale yellow-green which are its main attraction. It is a large plant, growing to 3 m (10 ft) high and more across but can be curtailed for some years by surreptitious pruning (eagerly undertaken by flower-arrangers!) until replacement by a smaller specimen becomes necessary. Although seen at its best in sunny, sheltered locations and requiring protection in northern England, it will tolerate quite heavy shade. The male form with its substantially longer catkins, is the better one to grow. Like *Garrya* the genus *Viburnum* provides a range of species of dense, rounded evergreen shrubs some of which are excellent plants in winter. *Viburnum tinus* (Laurustinus) is perhaps best known. Surviving as it does in the dusty relics of old shrubberies it has acquired an unfortunate reputation, together with privet, laurel and *Aucuba*, but it is an excellent solid background plant with the additional advantage of flowering freely in winter. The flowers are white or pale pink in flat heads. Although the foliage is an excellent filler in flower arrangements the flowers, unlike most winter flowers, are quite useless for picking, dropping in a matter of hours. There is a variegated form but the yellow variegation is not a good companion for the flowers and this plant always seems to attract more blackfly

The evergreen *Garrya elliptica* also produces its long catkins in winter

75

even than do nasturtiums and beans – or perhaps it merely displays them more conspicuously. *V. rhytidophyllum*, the leather-leaf viburnum is like Hilaire Belloc's little girl, either very, very good or horrid. In some gardens it makes a tall shrub 3–5 m (10–15 ft) high densely clothed in its very long wrinkled and very dark green leaves felted with brown hairs beneath. Its flowers are not inspiring, large umbels of a dirty brownish-white but in late summer the branches are weighed down with the huge clusters of red berries which follow. Elsewhere, however, it forms a thin straggling plant with the hanging leaves demanding more pity than admiration. Although perfectly hardy it is, I think, a plant for the warm humid gardens of south-western England. Elsewhere, although worth trying, it is safer to resort to the similar but more predictable *V. rhytidophylloides*, denser, paler and slightly smaller leaved than *V. rhytidophyllum*, a reliable plant but lacking the distinction of a well behaved specimen of the latter. Coming down the scale, *V. cinnamomifolium* makes a bright metre (3 ft) high mound of shiny green leaves and *V. davidii* is often only half this height although spreading 2 m (6 ft) or more across. *V. davidii* is worth growing for its foliage alone, a smoothly rounded low dome of dark green rather pleated leaves but, even in small gardens, it is worth planting a close group of one male and two or three females for the extra benefit of its clusters of dark blue berries.

There are many other evergreen

Viburnum davidii, a low shrub with pleated dark green leaves

shrubs – *Berberis, Cotoneaster, Escallonia* galore with the additional bonus of decorative flowers and fruits – and it would be too easy to overfill this book or a small garden by listing them all, but it is important to consider also the numerous lower evergreen plants which furnish the foreground of planting schemes and soften the transition from vertical banks of tall plant groups to the horizontal ground surface.

The hebes, or shrubby veronicas, are perhaps the most varied although only suitable for reasonably warm gardens. Most form quite compact, rounded plants but of very different colours and textures. *Hebe anomala* quickly grows to two metres (6 ft) or more with small dark green glossy foliage; *H. salicifolia* is of similar stature but of a very light green and with a softer, more spreading habit, while *H. cupressoides*, as its name suggests, closely resembles a blue-green conifer with its small leaves pressed closely against the stem. Whereas the first two have flowers in distinct white spikes (*H. salicifolia* being especially valuable in flowering into the autumn and even sporadically into winter), *H.*

cupressoides is scattered with tiny clusters of flowers rather like sugar-frosting. Although it grows as quickly and as tall as *H. amomala* and *H. salicifolia*, *Hebe cupressoides* becomes less attractive in middle age as its branches sag apart to disclose a dusty grey interior. This can be rectified by severe pruning in spring or by striking cuttings, ease of propagation being a pleasing feature of most hebes. Three smaller hebes showing still more variation are *H. albicans*, *H. armstrongii* and *H. x franciscana* 'Variegata'. *H. albicans* grows slowly to 40 cm (18 ins) or so high and is densely compact, with rounded leaves of blue-grey. It suffers two disadvantages however. One, a matter of opinion, is that its foliage is so neat, so well arranged and so immaculately firm that it does not look quite real. For the tidy-minded gardener it is ideal but to me it looks like an imitation of a plastic plant. The other fault, a matter of fact, is that the neat white spikes of flowers fade eventually to a soggy brown but refuse to leave the plant of their own volition. *H. armstrongii* is a very different plant. It is a whipcord hebe with minute leaves closely pressed to the stem giving the appearance of a golden conifer. The branches arch stiffly to give the plant a very interesting form and since the flowers are borne on young growth there is a distinct film of white flowers as though the plant were covered in frost. *H. franciscana* is another of the stiff, rounded, glossy-leaved hebes, its robustness of habit concealing the fact that, unlike the five species described above, it is not reliably hardy in central England. The variegated form, however, is sufficiently polished and bright as to be worth risking as it will survive most winters. This is the one plant which has all the cheer of variegated holly without the thorns! As it becomes hardier with age, presumably because the tender young shoots are lifted away from ground frosts, it is worth cossetting the plant for a year or two until it becomes established. More tender still are the larger flowered hybrids such as 'Amy', 'Midsummer Beauty', 'Autumn Beauty', 'La Seduisante' but even these will go through many winters unscathed. Some flower spikes are sufficiently long to merit comparison with small *Buddleja* spikes and the rich purple-crimson of the flowers is repeated in various degrees in the glossy foliage. Unlike the species which have a brief flowering season in early summer, most of the larger flowered hybrids flower in late summer or autumn and some will continue to flower sufficiently freely up to Christmas to merit consideration as winter-flowering plants. Although lacking the sumptuous richness of these hybrids, surely the most useful hebe is 'Mrs Winder'. It too has purple tinged foliage but a long slender shape. The flowers are borne in spikes of pale purple tipped with white and the habit, unlike any of the hebes mentioned above is of a loosely sprawling mound. It is an excellent plant for softening the hard edges of steps, walls, paths and again often flowers in mild spells throughout the winter.

Euonymus fortunei is an indispensible plant for the winter garden. Whereas the hebes are on the borderline of hardiness in Britain, *Euonymus fortunei* is as hardy as can be and will grow in dense shade, under trees and in other inhospitable situations. The plant usually seen is the variegated form of *E. f.* 'Radicans' and this is perhaps the most useful but also worth knowing are 'Kewensis' a dense, dark green carpet and 'Vegetus' with large pale glossy green leaves. *E. f.* 'Vegetus' is usually seen as a rounded shrub but it has modest climbing tendencies and can be trained along as a hedge or up as a climber on any rough surface. Unlike the smaller leaved forms it often fruits freely producing the typical orange spindle fruits although these are partly hidden by foliage.

For suitable acid soils there is of course the immense family of *Ericaceae* available with *Kalmia*, *Pieris*, *Leucothoë* and the mainstays of the family, *Rhododendron* and *Erica*. Rhododendrons are so numerous that it is difficult to know where to begin and as so many excellent books have been written on the genus it is perhaps advisable not to attempt to do them justice here. Mention should be made, however, of the Kurume Azaleas for their splendid horizontal layers of small glossy leaves often becoming purple in winter and of *Rhododendron orbiculare* with its greygreen neatly rounded leaves looking most unlike the dark polished leaves of

Heathers have few rivals for winter flowers and foliage: the heather garden at Wisley

most of its brethren. *Erica* species, too, have such a similarity amongst them that to mention the genus is almost enough. The neat rounded hummocks of fine needle-like leaves are common to all. The hummocks do, however, vary from the three metres or so (10 ft) of *E. arborea* 'Alpina' to the 15 cm (6 ins) of the weaker *E. carnea* (now *E. herbacea*) hybrids and from fresh pale green to dark purple green. The closely related genus *Calluna* do not vary so much in height, the only species being *C. vulgaris* but there are many, many cultivars offering a great variety of foliage colours in winter and flower colours in late summer. Although the golden leaved forms are very striking, my particular favourites for winter are the warm orange-red tinged foliage types such as 'Robert Chapman' and 'Sunset'. *Erica*, *calluna* and *daboecia* also have excellent ground-covering ability, smothering all but the largest seeded or perennial weeds.

Mention of the range of foliage colours in *Calluna* brings back to mind the point made earlier on the variety encompassed within the term 'evergreen', variety not only in colour but in form. Yucca, for example (*Y. filamentosa* being most widely grown) creates a useful accent amidst generally rounded plants and the enormous sword-like leaves of *Phormium tenax* are even more remarkable. On a smaller

scale the *Liriopes* have upright grasslike leaves which show up well against the brighter green domes of *Saxifraga moschata*. Some ornamental grasses are evergreen, two of the best being the bright green *Festuca eskia* and bluegrey *F. ovina* 'Glauca', both making hummocks 15 cm (6 in) or so high. Few tall grasses are evergreen but many remain attractive in winter with their leaves bleached to white or brown. *Stipa calamagrostis* and the still taller *S. gigantea* have persistent flower spikes and provide elegant points in the garden until late in the winter. Evergreen ferns from the strap-like *Phyllitis scolopendrium* (hart's tongue) to the much-divided fronds of *Polystichum setiferum* provide still further interesting varia-

tions of form and as a final note, the large palmate leaves of *Fatsia japonica* must not be overlooked – as if they could be with their glossy exotic appearance.

In colour the evergreens range from the greys and blues of *Santolina chamaecyparissus* and *Festuca ovina* 'Glauca' to the almost black foliage of *Ophiopogon planiscarpus* 'Nigrescens', from the purple of purple sage *Salvia* and *Viola labradorica* to the gold of the common golden privet (*Ligustrum ovalifolium* 'Aureum'). Variegated plants, of which the hollies have already been mentioned, provide a bright note and it is not surprising that *Elaeagnus pungens* 'Maculata' with its glossy gold-splashed leaves is a best seller among shrubs. Many silver or grey leaved plants are not very attractive in winter, their hairy leaves taking on a distinctly bedraggled appearance, but one plant must be singled out for praise – the silver leaved *Convolvulus cneorum*. A neatly rounded shrub usually growing to half-metre high and twice as much across (18 in by 3 ft) its leaves look almost as if painted with aluminium paint. Lest anyone has visions of gardens being enveloped by silver leaved bindweed it must be stressed that *C. cneorum* is a compact woody shrub with none of the bad habits of its invasive herbaceous brethren, sharing only the delight of their funnel-like flowers, white on opening but neatly pleated pink in bud. Like the hebes it is not absolutely hardy but small cuttings can be rooted and over-

Liriope spicata. The dark narrow leaves are a useful foil for other winter plants

79

wintered as an insurance against an exceptionally severe winter. It requires a well drained soil and the best plant I have ever seen trailed down a wall and thereby had the triple advantage of good drainage, shelter and excellent opportunity to flaunt its beauty.

Among the very low evergreens mention must be made briefly of *Iberis sempervirens* (perennial candytuft), a compact cushion of dark green especially if cut back after its white flowers in spring have faded. *Phlox subulata* is lower – 10 cm (3 in) or so – lighter green and looser but spreads into broad mats smothered with flowers of white, pink or red in spring. *Cerastium tomentosum*, a vigorous (often too vigorous) creeping plant has well behaved grey leaves and masses of delicate white flowers in summer while, as a total contrast there is now a considerable range of *Bergenia*, aptly called 'elephant's ears' by many people, with large, very glossy leaves often at their best in winter when they assume purple tints. The flowers of *Bergenia* are often borne in rather stubby spikes and are of a difficult magenta-pink colour but the newer forms have more open, branched inflorescences and in 'Silberlicht' the flowers are white, tinged pink. As well as being bold in foliage and flowering in winter *Bergenia* has still further merit in being virtually indestructable, growing in shade, on heavy clay soil and under shrubs with apparent ease. Lastly one of my favourite evergreens is the mossy saxifrage, *Saxifraga moschata*. It is not rare; it is not difficult and

perhaps as a result it suffers neglect from gardeners who consider it unworthy. Another problem is that it will soon grow into wide cushions and will quickly swamp slower alpine plants on rockeries but in most small gardens a fat cushion of bright green saxifrage bedecked in spring with its pale pink to red flowers would look far better than a few pieces of rubble and a scattering of alpine labels which seem to comprise so many rockeries. Although always attractive the cushions of dissected leaves are lifted quite out of the ordinary when fringed with white frost.

Foliage colour is, of course, well represented in the other great group of evergreen plants, the conifers but care is needed in their selection simply because they are so varied and so individually distinctive. Tall conifers are magnificent but too stiffly upright to be blended into small gardens and even the more rounded outlines of pines are only achieved after years as tight pyramids during which time they would overfill and overshadow a small garden. There are, however, hundreds of dwarf, slow growing and low growing conifers from which to choose although catalogue descriptions of what constitutes dwarf or slow growing vary almost as much as the plants. *Chamaecyparis lawsoniana* 'Elwoodii' which graces many a small rockery will grow to 4 m (12–15 ft) while *Chamaecyparis obtusa*, described in less reputable advertisements as 'dwarf' will grow quite rapidly and eventually reach 25 m (70 ft) or so! There are, however, much slower

growing forms of *C. obtusa* and generally speaking the longer the name the
shorter the plant. Poor old *C. obtusa*
'Juniperoides Compacta' rarely exceeds 30 cm (1 ft) in height. As with
other dwarf shrubs, the slower the
growth the more expensive will be a
plant of any given size so it pays always
to avoid cheap 'bargains' which are
often forms not truly dwarf and grafted
onto vigorous rootstocks to pump
them up to a saleable size as rapidly as
possible.

It is pointless to describe here every
low conifer which can be grown so I
list only ten to illustrate range.

Chamaecyparis obtusa has many excellent dwarf forms but *C. o.* 'Nana
Gracilis' is large enough to grow sensibly outside and has very dark green
foliage in the typical neat fan arrangement of the species making a rounded
lumpy hummock a metre (3 ft) or more
in height eventually. If that is too big
for your rock garden there are still
smaller forms but you would be better
advised to scrap such a small rock garden and grow the tree. *Pinus sylvestris*
'Beauvronensis' is a beautiful plant with
all the rugged quality of a full-scale
wind-swept pine. Left to its own devices it makes a loose dome but careful
removal of the lower branches will
reveal twisting trunks to make it a real
tree. *Tsuga canadensis* 'Pendula' is quite
different but equally full of character.
The needles are very dark green, straight
and broad in contrast to the pale blue-
green narrow twisted needles of the
pine, and the habit is gracefully weeping

*Juniperus subina
tamariscifolia*, a sea of
grey-green wavelets

Few plant groups
exceed conifers for
diversity of form and
colour. *Tsuga
cauadeusis* 'Pendula'
should not have its
form obscured by
crowded planting

Chamaecyparis obtusa,
a study in light and
shade

not from one point but from several to form a gently undulating mound with pendulous branches. It improves with age and although the improvement may make it too large for some situations – the largest plant I have ever seen was about 1½ m (5 ft) high and 4 m or so (nearly 15 ft) across – it will stay well within modest bounds for a very long time. All these are *dwarf* conifers, looking like small replicas of much larger trees and are best seen with a surrounding of very much lower plants.

Two conifers which blend with other plants are *Thuja orientalis* 'Elegantissima' and *Cryptomeria japonica* 'Elegans'. The former is an upright spire composed of many parallel ranks of flat branches. Its foliage, pale green fading to gold at the edges of the branches, is attractive at any time but in winter when the tips become burnished with bronze/

purple it is superb. The colouring is not only attractive in itself but serves to highlight the interesting form of the plant. *Cryptomeria japonica* 'Elegans' is a less inspiring but still very attractive plant. The juvenile form of a much larger timber tree it quickly loses its pyramidal shape taking on a billowing rounded form of soft pale green needles. In winter the exposed foliage becomes deep purple. This can become quite large, 5 m (17 ft) or more with a tendency to fall apart with age but it can be pruned quite satisfactorily if required or as a longer term measure cuttings will root more easily than most conifers and can be grown on as replacements.

Lastly among the conifers there are some excellent low junipers, not dwarf forms but with a horizontal habit which keeps them near to the ground. The best is undoubtedly *Juniperus sabina*

Evergreen planting in narrow drifts across the main line of vision gives a well-furnished appearance to the winter garden

side view

plan

'Tamariscifolia' with branches of narrow triangular outline spreading out as the plant grows to create a swirling effect difficult to describe but delightful to behold. It is usually 30 cm (1 ft) high and a metre (3 ft) across becoming much wider in time and is a light grey green in colour. *Juniperus conferta* is a much looser, softer and brighter green, equally attractive in its own way and mixing better with other plants than does the strict form of *J. sabina* var. *tamariscifolia*. Most dwarf junipers appear not to transplant very easily but *J. conferta* suffers more than most in this respect and is best bought as a small container-grown plant. *Juniperus horizontalis* has many good forms some ('Bar Harbor', 'Blue Rug' for example) being a striking blue-grey, but although *J. h.* 'Plumosa' has not such a marked colouring it does go a very good purple in winter. Most forms, too, have long narrow branches turning up at the tips giving an effect in a group reminiscent of lots of little wavelets lapping at a wall. (How fortunate that even comprehensive glossaries of botanical terms do not extend to include juniper branching habits!) The two other junipers on this list are rather larger. *Juniperus chinensis* 'Pfitzeriana' is spreading, vaguely similar to *J. sabina* var. *tamariscifolia* but on a much larger scale. Indeed although it is an excellent plant I include it here mainly to warn those who might see it listed elsewhere as a dwarf conifer for it will grow $2\frac{1}{2}$ m (8 ft) high and 6 m (20 ft) across and is not slow growing. It can be kept much smaller than this as it tolerates pruning but care is needed to ensure that the form of the plant is not lost. Any overlong branch should be shortened back to a point at which a smaller well-formed branch arises. Simply shearing the plant completely destroys its form. *Juniperus squamata* 'Meyeri' is included for the blueness of its steel blue needles. It is more upright than those mentioned earlier being slightly taller than wide and has an engaging habit of bearing its needles in broadly pyramidal clusters from each of which emerges the drooping snout of the growing tip. At maturity this habit results in an irregular outline, very distinct and attractive in winter.

Chapter 10

Decorative Stems

The strangely curling
bright yellow twigs
and stems of *Salix
matsudana* 'Tortuosa'
are most noticeable in
winter

ALTHOUGH a good proportion of evergreen plants in the garden is desirable, a point expounded later in this section, it should not be too substantial for fear of losing one of the most valuable attributes of the winter scene. At no other season are the form and colour of plant stems so well displayed.

The interest may lie in the quality of line, as with the slender beauty of *Acer palmatum* or the stumpy colonies of *Aralia chinensis*. It may result from the statuesque quality of the plant as with *Rhus typhina* (so aptly called stags horn sumach), *Corylus avellana* 'Contorta' and *Salix matsudana* 'Tortuosa'. Of these, *Rhus typhina* is a plant worthy of any garden having brilliant autumn colour in addition to its winter form. The cut-leaved form *R. t.* 'Laciniata' undergoes one of the most amazing transformations in the plant kingdom when, in late spring, the coarse curving branches are covered with large but very finely dissected leaves as graceful as any fern. This has just as good an autumn colour as the species but is less

vigorous, tending to sucker much less than the species, making it more suitable for garden use. Any cultivations which result in disturbance and breaking of the root system will, however, result in a sudden spate of suckering. Of the other two plants I would recommend the willow *Salix* despite its much larger size. The hazel *Corylus* is more picturesquely twisted and seldom exceeds 3 m (10 ft), usually half that, but the leaves of hazel being broad, the contortion which continues unabated to the tips of the plant gives the leaves an appearance of suffering from a heavy infestation of greenfly or a severe overdose of hormone weedkiller. The leaves are sufficiently dense that the contorted stems are revealed only in winter. The willow, too, has twisted leaves but these are slender, curved often almost into circles and serve only to emphasize the gracefully frothy nature of the whole plant. They are also sufficiently sparse to reveal much of the quality of the tree throughout the year. It grows quickly – I know of one twenty year old tree over 12 m

84

The peeling, cinnamon red stems of *Acer griseum* reveal their full grace in winter

(40 ft) tall but the plant is attractive from its earliest days, roots very easily from cuttings in water or planted directly in moist soil and is therefore no trouble to renew every ten years or so if necessary. Even young trees have the delightfully frightening habit portrayed in so many children's books of twisting branches drooping to clutch with gnarled fingers at babes in the wood.

Another aspect of winter stems is their colour, ranging from the waxy white of *Rubus cockburnianus* and pale yellow of *Cornus stolonifera* 'Flaviramea' to the dark purple of *Salix purpurea*. It is unfortunate for many gardeners that so many of the coloured stems are to be found among the willows *Salix* and dogwoods *Cornus* both of which require moist soils to give of their best and ample space for sufficient plants to create an effect. Each, it is true, can be pruned hard each year to produce a fresh crop of the brightest young stems, some will tolerate drier conditions and with a suitably contrasting background will be useful additions to the garden scene but what of free-draining gardens in drier regions?

Surprisingly few people seem familiar with *Ceanothus* x *delilianus* which, in addition to attractive flowers and foliage has stems varying from plum purple to red. Best of the group is 'Marie Simon' with red stems and the hard annual pruning necessary to keep the plants compact and floriferous also results in the brightest stems. For dry soils, too, the brooms are ideal. *Genista lydia* is a very low trailing plant, *Cytisus* x *kewensis* is taller – to about 50 cm (18 in) – and *Cytisus* x *praecox* is taller still but unlike most tall brooms remains fairly compact. All have good green stems but none is such a bright addition to the garden as *Genista hispanica* which may become 50 cm (18 in) tall and three times as wide although usually rather smaller. *Kerria japonica* also has bright green stems but unfortunately the plant most widespread in commerce is the double flowered form with a vigorous, upright habit. The single form must be sought, not because of any snobbery about the superiority of single flowers but because the plant has a more horizontal habit with slender zig-zag twigs. One advantage of the great interest in flower arranging, is that variegated plants are in demand and *Kerria japonica* 'Variegata' is now readily available. This white-variegated form is single-flowered and being slower growing than the type is even more suitable for smaller gardens. Many roses do well on drier soils and some have pleasantly although not brightly coloured stems. In *Rosa hugonis* for example, the stems are dull red. Because of the subdued colouring these shrub roses are best left unpruned to build up a mass of stems. One exception is *Rosa omeiensis* 'Pteracantha' in which the main winter interest is the display of large translucent red prickles best developed on young stems and hard regular pruning is therefore advisable.

Many effects with stems are subtle but never fail to appeal. We have, for

example, a large group of *Spiraea japonica* at one end of a shrub border. Its summer foliage is reasonable; I dislike the dusty pink flowers but in winter the close ranked vertical stems light up to warm orange-brown in the weak sunshine, earning redemption for the group on every sunny day. Much the same colouring can be seen at a lower level with the straggling stems of *Ceratostigma plumbaginoides* but this plant needs no excuse for retaining it.

While coloured twigged shrubs for well drained soils are not numerous, the same is not true of trees with ornamental bark. For many of these a light, slightly acid, leafy loam is ideal although many will thrive on alkaline soils including the best tree of all, *Acer griseum*. Many maples are attractive: *Acer grosseri* and the larger, laxer *A. pennsylvanicum* have snake-like bark striped with olive green, black and white; *A. palmatum* has bark varying from silver-grey to the surprisingly bright pink of *A. p.* 'Senkaki' but *A. griseum* has peeling

bright orange bark translucent in sunshine and with the soft pink of its expanding leaves (which does not clash with the orange!) the neat summer foliage and brilliant autumn colour it has few rivals at the top of the list. When one adds that it grows well even on chalk soils its competitors fade away. Alas! It is difficult to propagate and therefore expensive to buy but how much is half a century of increasing pleasure worth? (It is anticipated that the observer, not the tree, will weaken within fifty years of the purchase!) Other trees of course exist. *Prunus serrula* has spectacular polished bark of orange-brown; birches, *Betula* including our native silver birch are very attractive varying from the whiter than white of *B. papyrifera*, through the creamy bark of *B. ermanii*, the more definite orange of *B. maximowiczii* to the delightful shaggy brown of *B. nigra*. All are fast growing, slender, open-headed trees which might well find a place in shade-lovers' gardens but the dense surface roots will eventually make cultivation of other plants beneath the birch difficult. *Stewartia pseudocamellia* is another beautiful tree in many respects: its foliage, horizontal branching, autumn colour and late summer white flowers are all deserving of praise but not least of its attributes is the bark, flaking in patches like a slender plane tree to create a mosaic of cream and brown. A similar pattern, although not developing for many years, occurs on *Cornus kousa* another immensely useful small tree.

Winter Flowers

TO SOME degree enjoying a garden in winter requires a new outlook rather than new plants. The garden is not a blaze of salvias or dahlias but if one is prepared to appreciate beauty of form, subtle colouring of stems, elegance of twig or bud then winter can be enjoyed more fully. There are, however, flowers to be had and flowers in plenty. It took much snipping to reduce the following list to less than fifty plants and even then it was necessary to avoid any mention of bulbs which have a chapter to themselves elsewhere. Neither have I included *Rhododendron* because, although many are hardy plants and flower from Christmas onwards, the flowers themselves are not hardy. A sharp frost reduces them to pulp and although there are many more buds to open, I seem more often dismayed by the pulp than delighted by the promise.

The following plants are largely trouble free, hardy (unless otherwise noted) and have their main flowering season within the months November to February. There are many other plants, of course, which extend into winter. *Schizostylis* flowers in October often well into November, even my sweet peas this year were presentable in mid-November and the spring-flowering quinces (*Chaenomeles*) usually produce a flower or two all winter long but these are for a book, not a chapter on winter gardens.

When does winter begin? *Arbutus unedo* can hardly be termed a winter-flowering plant but to me the fat white bells appearing in the garden among blazing colours of autumn flowers and foliage signifies the beginning of the end. Like many cold season flowers the *Arbutus* has a prolonged display frequently flowering into the new year while on nearby shoots the round spiky red fruits which give the plant its common name of strawberry tree ripen where last year's flowers were borne. Although a member of the great family *Ericaceae* and sharing a strong family likeness with *Leucothöe*, *Pieris* and *Zenobia* the *Arbutus* grows perfectly well on chalky soils. Although by our definition not winter flowering, it is ever-

Opposite:
Winter flowers. The scented flowers of witchhazel are frail only in appearance

Inset:
Mahonia japonica also has fragrant flowers, often in a setting of brilliant leaves

green with excellent glossy foliage. The bark is not of the quality of the spring-flowering *A. andrachne* or *A.* x *andrachnoides* which have smooth glowing orange bark but as it is many, many years before the *Arbutus* leave their shrubby childhood for tree status to reveal the bark, *A. unedo* is more valuable for its reliable late flowering.

The next deeply philosophical question engendered by winter flowering plants is 'when is a flower not a flower?'. I have deliberately avoided mention of plants producing only sporadic flowers in winter but several truly winter flowering plants take such a long time to develop and to lose their flowers that it is very difficult to ascertain whether they are in flower or not. *Erica herbacea* (*E. carnea*) for example shows clear

evidence of flower buds by late summer and these expand gradually throughout the autumn and winter. Long before Christmas one has the impression that 'Springwood White', one of the most vigorous and one of the best cultivars of *E. herbacea*, is in full flower but that the flowers are not as good as usual. In fact it is a month or more after Christmas that the flowers are truly open and as clear a white as one remembered from other years. This long season of interest, spread even further by grouping early and late flowering cultivars, combined with the fresh green weed smothering foliage account for much of this heather's great popularity. Like *Arbutus* and unlike almost all other heathers, *E. herbacea* will grow on chalk soils, but grows much more success-

Christmas rose lightens a dark corner. Its dark foliage will later support small lilies or colchicums

fully if the chalk soil has liberal quantities of humus worked into it. Simultaneously with the heather *Garrya elliptica* produces its tight green buds in late summer and these enlarge from late November to February forming graceful pendant catkins of pale yellow green. This shrub has already been mentioned as an evergreen of quality and described more fully in that section.

Even more protracted a display can be seen with *Helleborus foetidus*. My plants came from Devon two years ago and by October the terminal growth, paler green and more congested than usual, indicated the presence of flower buds. By December the garden diary excitedly proclaimed '*Helleborus foetidus* in flower!' for it had several little green globes. In January it had even more then apparent disaster. One very frosty morning poor *H. f.* had collapsed into a pathetic heap – I thought I must have obtained a tender clone suited only to the south-western counties – but by lunch time it had undergone a miraculous recovery and has many times since collapsed and resurrected itself. By February most of the little globes were opening to wider cups of beautiful pale green and the diary added an exclamation mark: '*Helleborus foetidus* still in flower!!' March and April passed. New shoots arose from the base and the widespread inflorescence was still impeccable. I had exhausted the supply of exclamation marks. In July the new shoots had topped the old inflorescence and as the latter was now shedding seed it was reluctantly removed to make way

for the new growth. Not everyone will like *Helleborus foetidus* (thank goodness!). I have heard its finely cut dark green leaves and pale green flowers described as 'evil' but it increases in popularity despite its common name of stinking hellebore, and it deserves to be very widely planted.

Helleborus niger, the Christmas rose is more commonly known but often disappointing. It is a variable plant and any effort expended in searching out a floriferous clone with long stemmed well formed pure white flowers is effort well spent. It flowers sporadically throughout the year but with greater profusion in January and February and appears to thrive on neglect. Heavy alkaline soil seems to be ideal for in the non-gravelly parts of our garden with a foot of slightly sticky soil over chalk it seeds freely even though growing under hawthorn, ash and yew. In other gardens with apparently much better soils I have seen it repeatedly reintroduced, failing gradually each time. Another indeterminate flower is the so-called autumn cherry, *Prunus subhirtella* 'Autumnalis' which flowers not much in autumn but sporadically from November to April. It is a slender, quite fast growing tree but one of moderate dimensions. Each autumn its branches are clothed with masses of buds and with each spell of good weather the tree is lightly sprinkled with small pink flowers, to be ruined by the next heavy frost or rain. Eventually when spring at last arrives there is a final flourish before the leaves

appear. It is never weighed down with blossom, is much better against a dark background than against the sky but is a tree high on the list for inclusion in small gardens. Lastly among the longest flowering of winter plants – and never to be included in the same view as the cherry – is *Jasminum nudiflorum*, starting well before Christmas and continuing well into February and often into March. This winter jasmine is among the brightest flowers especially when the bright yellow is seen against its own massed green stems. The one difficulty is its growth habit. Although frequently listed as a climber it is more accurately described as a flopper. It can be trained up as a rather straggling wall plant, is better finding its way through other large shrubs and better still left to grow into a tumbling mound, cutting back the skirt each year to prevent rooting at the tips and cutting back severely from time to time to regenerate the whole plant.

Another characteristic of many winter flowers and another good reason for planting near the house is their delightful perfume. In some the scent is not only sweet but carried for long distances. The witchhazel, *Hamamelis mollis* is outstanding in this respect. A beautiful plant in all seasons it excels itself in late December and January when the spidery flowers expand to outline the branch structure in pale yellow. Although fragile in appearance the flowers emerge unscathed from snow or frost and are beautifully scented. In sunny weather, and anyone with a witch-hazel will know that few Januaries pass without a scattering of sunny days, the scent pervades the surrounding garden. Each year a group of students advance, noses first, on a witch hazel planted at the far side of a large lawn and most are able to detect the scent quite clearly at twenty five metres (75–80 ft). To grow well it requires an acid or neutral leafy soil and adequate moisture but although I am generally in favour of growing plants suited to the native soil of a garden, I make an exception in thinking that half a witch hazel is better than none and would recommend it for any garden given generous preparation of the planting hole. Its form does not lend itself to small gardens, being a low-branching spreading plant 6 m (20 ft) or more across and half as high but it is slow growing (too slow when one first purchases a very expensive twig of a new plant) and will be many years outgrowing a square metre or so. Most gardening books describe *Hamamelis* as intolerant of pruning but this simply implies that it will not readily produce new shoots if cut back. It does not mean that snipping off a few twigs for the house will result in instant death of the plant and we have occasionally removed branches 5–7 cm (2–3 ins) diameter from large plants with no trouble. The witch hazel is therefore the sort of obliging plant which, planted in a small garden, will remain a delightful small shrub for many years and, by removal of whole branches as they intrude beyond their alloted space, can eventually form spreading canopies beneath

Opposite:
Iris unguicularis is variable. Here it flowers with early narcissus in March

Inset:
Helleborus foetidus: six months of flowers, twelve months of elegant leaves, and always striking in foliage

which small bulbs, ground cover plants or tired gardeners can shelter. There are several named forms and the flowering season can be extended with the later flowering *H. vernalis* and *H. japonica* (February–March) with *H. japonica* 'Flavopurpurascens' sometimes extending into April but none is so beautiful as the ordinary *H. mollis* unless, perhaps, one prefers the warmer orange flowers of the *H. mollis* x *H. japonica* hybrid *H.* x *intermedia* 'Jelena'.

Although no match for witch hazels in floral beauty the genus *Sarcococca* are amazing examples of 'long-distance' perfumes and I am always surprised that they are not more widely grown. My favourite is *S. ruscifolia*. Although not the most strongly scented it has beautifully polished dark green slender leaves on long arching branches and when it flowers, at much the same time as *Hamamellis mollis* the tiny white flowers announce their presence by a strong vanilla-like perfume. It may be that our *S. ruscifolia* is a fraud and that its habit is due to its very shaded situation at the roots of some overgrown evergreens because other plants received more recently from usually reliable nurseries have been duller and more compact. If this is so, I would recommend planting only in shady situations to accentuate the beauty of the plant. Much stiffer, more closely suckering, paler and distinctly red-tinted in the stem is *S. hookerana* 'Digyna'. This is more widely grown than is *S. ruscifolia* and I had often wondered why anyone (including our-

selves!) grew it at all until last year when going into the office I inhaled a wondrous perfume. Determined to find the source I tramped around the garden and finally tracked down *S. hookerana* 'Digyna' nearly a hundred metres away at the far side of a dense planting of holly, witch hazel, birch and other tall plants! This must have been caused by unusual weather conditions as I have not noticed the occurrence before or since but *S. hookerana* 'Digyna' is a plant of great value for its pervasive scent. All the *Sarcococca* species grow to about 0.5–1 m (2 ft or so) and spread slowly by suckers. They will grow slowly but surely in shade including the dry, rooty, shade of trees.

Mahonia japonica is another superb plant which tolerates shade and dry soils but grows much better elsewhere. It would still be widely grown if it never flowered, possessing as it does long pinnate spiky leaves of polished green becoming more richly coloured in winter and held in bold terminal rosettes. It is, however, even more richly endowed for in each rosette nestles a whorl of flower spikes opening to strongly scented yellow flowers. A few flowers open quite early, even in November, but the main season is after Christmas from late January to early March. The virtues of *M. lomariifolia* and hybrids from it, such as 'Charity' are often extolled and they are certainly more architectural in form and more spectacular in leaf than *M. japonica* but the flowers are inferior: I much prefer the looser stems broader richly coloured leaves and abundant flowers of *M. japonica*.

The wintersweet *Chimonanthus praecox* (*C. fragrans*) is a problem. Its flowers are attractive on close inspection, the scent is wonderful and twigs for the house are a great joy but it lacks other distinction and is not suitable, therefore, for small gardens. It makes a large, rather untidy shrub but can be (and usually is) trained against a wall pruning the new growth immediately after flowering to produce a fresh crop of shoots which, in a good summer, will ripen and form flower buds. Too hard a pruning of older wood will produce vigorous shoots which usually fail to flower. Despite its apparent difficulties we had one plant in a crevice between a north-facing wall and a path which scarcely grew but flowered abundantly every year until, regretfully, the wall became a garage door and the plant was dispatched to retire happily in Devon

Prunus subhirtella 'autumnalis' needs a dark background to be seen at its best. It may flower from October to April

where it now grows but has not yet flowered. One of the shrubby honeysuckles, *Lonicera fragrantissima*, is another large shrub with small but pleasantly scented flowers. It is, however a neat shrub, upright and smoothly rounded with good grey-green foliage, evergreen in the milder counties. Although never ostentatious it is useful as a background plant with its scented flowers as a bonus.

On a very different scale to all these shrubs, room can be found in any garden for violets and *Iris unguicularis* (*I. stylosa*). The sweet violets of the flower trade are fat, opulent flowers requiring mountains of humus, reservoirs of water and gardeners who, when they are not controlling red spider mite on violets are lifting, dividing and replanting violets or burning virus infected violets. The same plants, however, the ordinary *Viola odora*, can be left to fend for themselves producing mats of bright green leaves and a succession of small but still sweetly scented flowers throughout the winter. *Iris unguicularis* is a flower for the house. The plant is a tangle of thin leaves which insist on dying back at the tips and although it is said to require a hot dry position I would not give it a hot dry *conspicuous* position: there are other plants more decorative for such a valuable spot. The iris will however grow and flower (perhaps rather less freely) in most situations and can usually be found an out of the way spot to produce its frail and beautiful scented flowers. It is a variable plant, in colour from ashy white to

deep lavender, in leaf from narrow to wide, short to tall, and in flower production from generous to sparse, early, sporadic or late so, as with *Helleborus niger*, do look for a good form. Ours flowers sporadically but mainly in February and March and I should like to find an earlier flowered form.

From the small to the luxuriously large, *Acacia dealbata* can be grown in at least half of Britain in sheltered situations. It is a very fast-growing tree often putting on a metre or more (5–6 ft) in a year but the growth is slender and light, like a birch and the plant can easily be kept in bounds by drastic pruning. Also it will not outgrow its shelter for any length of time being cut back by cold winters. The foliage is lacy and pale grey-green and the flowers, masses of tiny yellow puff balls commonly known as 'mimosa' open in February and are very fragrant.

Lastly but certainly not least is a small group of plants which qualify both as fragrant and as very long flowering, the winter-flowering *Viburnum* species. *Viburnum tinus*, mentioned earlier as an evergreen, is certainly long flowering but only faintly and rather unpleasantly scented. *V. foetens* (foetens – stinking – applies to the bruised wood, not the flowers) is scented although not long lasting, but *V. farreri* (*V. fragrans*) – its offspring *V.* x *bodnantense* and clonal selections such as 'Dawn' are very fragrant and produced from November to February. *V.* x *bodnantense* is the stronger plant, has larger, deeper pink flowers and is now the more commonly planted.

There is a very good dwarf form of the species, however. *V. farreri* 'Nana' makes a neat rounded dome about half-metre (18 ins) high with very good autumn colour. I cannot speak for its flowering qualities: our plants grew for many years behind a yew hedge and under a cedar, not very propitious for flowers, and succeeded in producing a scattering of flowers each year. They have now been moved to a more open situation and I am awaiting their activities in the next year or two with great interest: it may be that, as with the dwarf *Forsythia*, low growth is at the expense of flowers but even if this proves to be the case we shall keep *V. farreri* 'Nana' for its neat growth, autumn colour and occasional flowers.

As *V.* x *bodnantense* fades, *V.* 'Park Farm Hybrid', looking like a robust *V.* x. *burkwoodii* and just as heavily scented, begins the long list of late winter flowering plants which merge the season imperceptibly into spring. *Cornus mas*, neatly rounded but eventually very large, starts to produce its fluffy yellow globes in January, but is at its best in February–March as is *Parrotia persica* (more spectacular in autumn foliage than in its rich red but sparse witch hazel-like flowers). As these finish *Corylopsia pauciflora* produces its primrose yellow flowers on slender twigs and *Daphne odora* finally opens its reserve of flower buds from a store which has been meagrely dispensed for two or three months previously: meagrely but

99

not unnoticed as the flowers are power-fully fragrant. Where the shelter of a wall can be provided the creamy white flowers of *Abeliophyllum distichum* and the bright yellow but concealed *Azara microphylla* are also fragrant in Febru-ary. *Forsythia* usually signifies spring but *F. giraldiana* flowers with less deter-mined yellowness in February often two weeks before *F. x intermedia* goes into battle with flowering currant and pink flowering peach. On a lower note, both in colour and stature, *Pulmonaria angustifolia* – which looks interested in flowering from January onwards – finally opens its pink and blue flowers in early March but it will provide good mottled foliage over a long period to earn its place in the garden.

Herbaceous plants, too, can make their own subtle contribution to the winter garden for many have compact shapes covered with the rusty brown remains of last season's leaves and often attractive seedheads. *Sedum spectabile* is very useful in this respect. Indeed were it not for the generous contribution which its flowers make to butterflies I would consider it more attractive in winter than in its more corpulent pale green summer state. The *Achillea* species too, with their flat plates of seed-heads, and the spikes of *Aruncus sylvester* are attractive while *Anaphalis nubigena* keeps its papery white flowers almost indefinitely to create a lighter note. Grasses extend the range of winter colour from bleached white to smoky brown, grey and purple. Many other plants are only marginally less attractive

and herbaceous borders at a distance from the windows of the house could often be left until late winter for the sake of the general form before cutting down in preparation for a new year. Even as the dead remains are removed to the bonfire winter merges into spring with the emergence of those few trusty herbaceous plants which regularly send up leaves far in advance of their neigh-bours. Were the *Hemerocallis* not so valuable for their weed-smothering propensities, their good foliage and their abundant flowers in an ever increasing range of colour they would still be invaluable components of any planting scheme for the sake of the fresh green shoots often appearing in January. Border *Phlox* too are early starters with foliage ranging from pale green to purple while oriental poppy, and others extend the range.

Arrangement of the garden for winter

Perhaps more than at any other time of year the siting of plants in winter is of vital importance. With so much vege-tation gone one must be sure that the remnants are not dotted about at ran-dom and that plants with attractive stems are not lost in a tangle of plants less attractive in winter. Evergreens and the denser deciduous plants should provide substantial enclosure and, if this can be made to wrap around the north side of the boundary it will shelter from the coldest winds and allow full exposure to sun. Given these conditions it is surprising how often one can enjoy a cup of coffee in the garden even in January and February among the scents of winter flowers. A good backdrop is also important to display to their best the small pale flowers, *Viburnum* and *Cornus mas* in particular. Plants grouped in masses emphasize the presence of flowers but care must be taken as the two predominant winter flower colours are pink and yellow – not good companions – and even the yellows do not always associate well as anyone who has ever planted winter aconites and yellow crocus together will realize! Plants with decorative bark should be placed where they catch the afternoon rays of the sun to show them at their best and the small trees should, of course, be well clear of general shrub groups to reveal their full beauty. With low evergreen plants one good technique is to use them in long drifts perpendicular to the main line of vision making the garden look well furnished but leaving concealed areas for summer-growing plants. Of the low plants some are best seen against the dark earth or shadows (snowdrops and Christmas roses for example), some crocus require support among low planting while *Cyclamen coum* requires a very low ground cover or a surfacing of pine needles or grit to prevent the flowers being splashed.

Most important in placing or grouping of winter plants is to keep them within easy view of the main windows of the house and on the main daily routes through the garden, from back door to garage or front door to the gate. Generosity is also most warmly received at this cold time of year: my journey to work through a grey traffic-splashed world is made infinitely brighter every time I pass an enormous old witch hazel in full flower. Making the most of your garden means that countless others will share in your delight.

Part Four
The Flowery Mead

Chapter 12

Some Definitions

FROM mediaeval manuscripts it would appear that the early English gardens were very different from those of today. Turf was brought in from the meadows, beaten out very thinly and allowed to grow with all its richness of wild plants to form a 'flowery mead'. As the coarser grasses gradually smothered more attractive plants the whole garden would be stripped and re-turfed. Gradually, we must surmise, the flowers were introduced in their own right and the grasses weeded out to reappear some centuries later as the ornamental lawn.

The concept of a flowery mead can still be employed directly in larger gardens by planting narcissus, tulip, crocus and other bulbs in rough grass. Because the grass is cut only once or twice a year after the bulb foliage has died down, many wild flowers will also increase gradually to enrich the turf and one can, of course, hasten the enrichment by deliberate planting. We have introduced primroses and cowslips beneath fruit trees and I have seen *Phlox subulata* and *Cerastium tomentosum*

thriving on dry grassy banks and looking very attractive. In small areas, however, long grass looks dishevilled rather than natural and, much as the appeal of flower-strewn chalk downland or alpine meadows lingers in our memories, some substitute must be found in small gardens. Many great gardeners have paved the way by showing how the best traditions of the old English cottage garden can be modified to suit new gardens and to take advantage of the great range of plants now available to us by mingling plants in a very intimate and fine textured planting to produce a new flowery mead. These twentieth century plantings can be broadly categorized in three groups, those relying mainly on flowers, foliage and form respectively, although as in any categorization there are no hard and fast divisions.

The first type (the 'flowery flowery mead') is similar to the traditional concept of an herbaceous border except that, instead of being planted with distinct clumps of many different plants, the choice of plants is more restricted

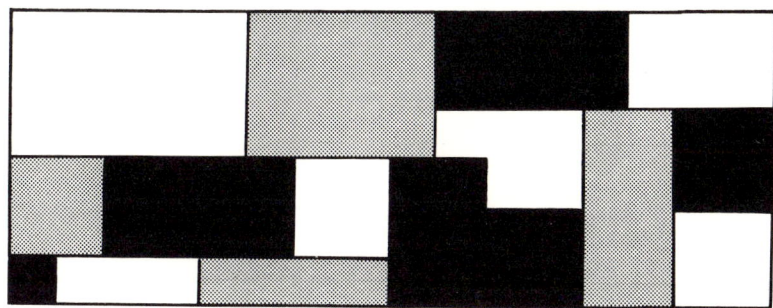

institutional planting in square blocks

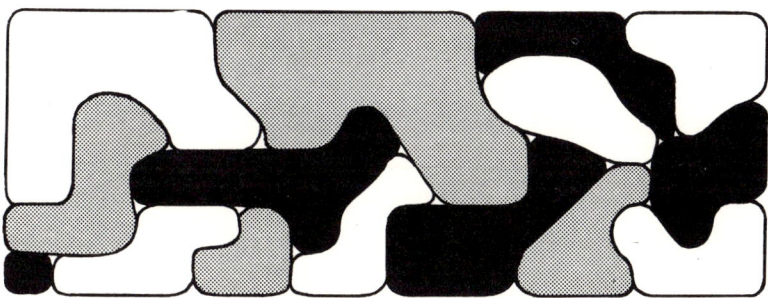

less rigid drifts as in typical herbaceous border

complete intermingling of plants – 'the flowery mead'

Three different ways
of grouping plants:
modern gardens rely
more and more on
intimate mingling of
plants to create a
relaxed and luxuriant
appearance

and each species mingled with every other throughout the whole border. In this way the whole area is sprinkled with the flowers of one or two species to be replaced gradually by other species as they fade. Such borders can provide delightful examples of colour harmonies and the season of interest can be extended still further by carpeting bulbs among the herbaceous plants but they lack permanent substance. Like other herbaceous borders they are seen at their best in large gardens where trees and shrubs elsewhere in the garden give sufficient height and substance.

The second and more commonly seen example often has a good display of flowers but these are seen as second in importance to the more permanent effect of foliage. Instead of geraniums, columbines, phlox, poppies, anemones and annuals the mainstay of the planting would be the low evergreens – lavender, sage, *Santolina*, *Bergenia*. The height of planting may be varied by incorporating bold yuccas, *Fatsia* and rosemary but the overall effect is of a gently undulating carpet of varying shades of green enlivened here and there by flowers. Good examples of this type of planting are of course effective throughout the year and give me the same sort of pleasure that I derive from watching the sea, with little waves uniting to form peaks, subsiding and reforming in an ever changing pattern. Such plantings are ideal for small borders in rectangular town gardens where it is important that the garden reflects its surroundings but that the hard

straight edges should be softened. A garden of straight lines need not be uninteresting nor formal!

The third type is really an extension of the other two with shrubs or small trees playing a more important role. In public places and large gardens shrubs and trees alone provide sufficient variety of form and texture but in small gardens each shrub takes too much room in proportion to the whole garden and it is much better to space the shrubs more widely and to carpet the ground between with lower plants. Thus the third type of planting has the variation in height increased by grouping of taller shrubs at intervals with stretches of flowery mead in the bays thus created and, occasionally, a taller tree or shrub brought to the fore with the lower flowering plants nestling around the base of its stems. Such plantings, folded around a small paved area or lawn could provide the whole structure of a small garden and it is for this reason that I so frequently use the word 'planting' rather than 'beds' and 'borders' which seem to suggest little bits of scattered planting to the detriment of the garden as a whole.

A general scheme for such a garden would include a few tall shrubs or small trees with their leaves well above the lower plants nestling beneath and some long drifts of low evergreens or twiggy shrubs for winter interest and permanent form. In the bays between these shrubs and beneath the larger plants the ground would be carpeted in late winter and in spring with masses of

Opposite:
The flowery mead.
Welsh poppy,
bluebell, *Viola
cornuta* and hardy
geraniums create
three months of
floral beauty at
Hidcote Manor

dwarf bulbs to be followed by herbaceous flowering and foliage plants giving an ever changing but permanently satisfying scene. Although it is possible to summarize such a plan for making the most of your garden in a few words it must be emphasized again that with the unlimited possibilities of selecting and arranging plants to suit varying soils, situations and tastes there is no danger of producing a stereotyped 'everyman's garden', a disaster too dreadful to contemplate.

What plants to choose? The choice is, of course, enormous but it is the express purpose of this book to be selective and to advise rather than be comprehensive and confuse. I give below some recommendations first for trees and shrubs – the permanent backbone – then for bulbs – so temporary yet collectively, with their ability to push up among other plants, produce such exquisite flowers and then to fade away, so important – and finally herbaceous plants, climbers and the more permanently useful 'temporary' plants, the annuals and tender perennials. For those seeking a wider choice there are of course many excellent books, some running to several volumes, on each of these plant types.

Inset:
Sorbus, 'Joseph Rock' has a graceful form and persistent soft yellow fruit

Opposite:
Sorbus sargentiana, a bold shrubby tree for a prominent position

Chapter 13

Trees and Shrubs

THESE are in all senses the high points of the garden and must be selected with care. There is scarcely a garden which could not be improved by the additional height afforded by their presence and if you are unable to lie in the dappled shade of a leafy canopy then you should search the following list with great care. If there is room for only one larger plant, as is often the case in very small gardens, then winter interest is particularly important and I would especially recommend the maples, cherries and so on mentioned in Chapter 10, or perhaps *Prunus subhirtella* 'Pendula' if an elegant small weeping tree is required. *Amelanchier laevis* is also a favourite. Its leaves turn from translucent bronze to pale green as they expand and then to brilliant crimson with some yellow and orange in the autumn. The flowers which appear with the new leaves are white, delicate and very short lived, followed by red fruits, also short lived as they are much loved by birds, and in winter the bark is a pleasant silvery grey. This is a variable plant and usually

needs some persuading to forsake a shrubby habit and develop into a tree but once persuaded the form of the tree is excellent. Many mountain ash *Sorbus* are beautiful and I am especially fond of *S.* 'Joseph Rock' and *S. sargentiana*. The first is a slighter form of our native rowan but with brilliant red autumn colour and bright yellow fruits which persist for a considerable time. *Sorbus sargentiana* looks more like a sumach than a sorbus. It has immense leaves on thick, sparsely branched twigs which, in winter, could quite easily be mistaken for horse-chestnut, such is the size of the glossy terminal bud. The autumn colour is again excellent (mainly orange) and the huge inflorescences of typical mountain ash white flowers are followed by scarlet fruits in trusses 20 cm (8 in) or more across. Although the fruit is the same colour as that of the ordinary mountain ash and one would expect it to disappear rapidly it does, in fact, persist. I have a theory that birds simply do not believe their eyes when they see the huge trusses because, when, eventually, a more inquisitive than

Prunus subhirtella
'Pendula', an excellent
choice where there is
room for only one
tree

Sorbus sargentiana, a bold plant in stem, leaf and fruit, with brilliant autumn colour

for initial – and perhaps permanent – effect.

Rosa moyesii is not the fastest growing shrub and neither is it the most attractive plant in winter, being rather too gaunt and stiff but it has good foliage, excellent deep red single flowers and magnificent long red hips in autumn, often persisting into winter. Our plant thinks it is a tree and is now about 3.5 m (12 ft) tall and half as much across. Despite its minor deficiencies it is an excellent plant for height and is especially suitable for people only half persuaded by my argument that height, overhead canopy and shade are essential to the enjoyment of a garden. You will be converted. *Buddleja davidii*, mentioned in Chapter 2, and the more attractive *B. fallowiana* also suffer from thin, stiff branching but are very quick growing and make ideal temporary trees or, with regular pruning, permanent large shrubs. *Viburnum* x *bodnantense*, so admirable in its long winter flowering season is an even tighter bundle of straight sticks in adolescence but at maturity it opens up well and I have often toyed with the idea of thinning stems and tying them down to encourage premature middle age spread. The winter flowers, orange-brown stems, pleasant foliage purple tinged in autumn make it a very useful plant of sufficient yet limited height. Lastly and in the same breath, lilac *Syringa* and mock orange *Philadelphus* deserve notice. Perhaps simultaneous treatment is at the risk of confusion as mock orange is commonly known –

average thrush samples a berry, word quickly gets around and the plant is stripped virtually overnight and one sees dozens of overweight birds staggering about croaking feebly or lying propped against a suitable branch. *S. sargentiana* may sound gross, I think perhaps it is gross, but nicely so.

The only problem with most small trees is that they are too small for too long and unless one is prepared to group several to form a mini-spinney they are not effectively substantial for the first five years or so. They are worth growing for their bark, flowers, foliage or fruit seen at close range but in a small garden and especially for those poor people who seldom stay in one place as long as five years, it is wise to invest in some faster growing tall shrubs

quite unaccountably – as 'syringa' and the lilac is, of course, correctly known as *Syringa vulgaris*. Nevertheless, both are initially quick growing (mock-orange the more so) both flower in summer and both are delightfully scented. Both are also widely planted and grossly mistreated. Lilac is the earlier to flower, usually in May, and at maturity has a more interesting form. To encourage it to adopt a tree form any new growths from the base should be cut away leaving a few main stems to branch as they will. Older branches flower much more readily so this treatment will also result in a more floriferous plant. As the cultivars of lilac, single or double in many shades of red, purple, lavender, white and even cream, are budded onto common lilac stocks care must be taken to prevent suckering and the plant should never be sheared. So often one sees a tightly clipped mound of suckers with sparse mildewed leaves of no ornamental value whatsoever. Even privet would look better in such circumstances. The same brutal treatment is often accorded to mock orange except that, the young stems of mock orange being stouter, the plant is often sawn off rather than sheared. Here there is even less excuse for maltreatment since there are several low-growing species and varieties of *Philadelphus* which form attractive rounded plants without the effort wasted in cutting back. *Philadelphus microphyllus* and *P.* 'Manteau d'Hermine' are good examples. 'Sybile' is more spreading but

heavily scented. For the present purpose though, as a small tree, 'Belle Etoile' is unsurpassed. Vigorous, floriferous and very heavily scented it quickly grows to 3 m (10 ft) or more if left unpruned. Lilacs associate well with paeonies and tulips both in colour and season but mock orange, flowering as it does in late June or early July when the early summer peak of flowering is past, can flower in isolated splendour and usefully fill the gap between the bulbs, azaleas, lupins and other early flowers and the mainstay of late summer plants.

Lower shrubs are legion and many have been mentioned in the section on evergreens in Chapter 9 but mention must be made of the herbs – lavender, rue, sage, santolina, rosemary and thyme for their neatly rounded shapes in various shades of blue/green from silvery-grey to purple. All tolerate very severe cutting back and can therefore be kept neat and within bounds indefinitely. In milder areas the small leaved myrtle, *Myrtus communis* 'Tarentina' forms a compact rounded shrub of very dark green. It flowers rather later than common myrtle and the flowers frequently fail to open but the pinkish buds, produced in great profusion, are themselves attractive in autumn and winter, so any opening of the white flowers is a welcome bonus.

The genus *Hebe* has already been mentioned as has the invaluable *Euonymus radicans*. *Cistus* come within the same general size range from the 30 cm (1 ft) *C. clusii* to the 2 m (6 ft) plus *C. x cyprius*, my own favourite being *C.*

corbariensis, usually about 50 cm (18 ins) tall. The *Cistus* are doubly useful in flowering prolifically in July – not an easy month – and in having with a few exceptions dense foliage of dark wrinkled green. However they are not utterly hardy and do not respond well to pruning so they will eventually either be killed in a severe winter or continue to grow into an all-engulfing mound at the expense of surroudning plants. It is wise, therefore, to keep a small stock of plants rooted from midsummer cuttings as replacements for either eventuality.

Other low evergreens include *Alyssum* (*A. saxatile* 'Citrinum' is a good pale yellow which combines well with *Aubrieta* and *Arabis*) with floppy greyish leaves, *Heuchera* with dark leaves attractively marbled with silver, thrift (*Armeria*) with hummocks of grassy dark green foliage, *Waldsteinia ternata* like a compact yellow flowering strawberry, *Lamium maculatum* and of course *Bergenia*. Pinks *Dianthus* make useful grey-leaved mats. There are many excellent named forms but as they are often not long lived I once grew some plants from a packet of mixed seed and now continue selected forms from cuttings taken after flowering, a cheap and very satisfactory way of raising large numbers of plants. Many other plants remain unmentioned but the above list includes some good and readily available plants for many soils and situations.

With a few strategically placed small trees or large shrubs and drifts of low evergreens and other shrubs meandering between and around them the garden will appear well-furnished all year long. The spaces between the groups can then be filled with bulbs, herbaceous and temporary plants for colour, remembering always that the evergreen background will have its own floral tribute to provide in due season.

Chapter 14

Bulbs

THERE are many bulbous plants ideally suited to the flowery mead and they may conveniently be grouped under two headings, those (mainly dwarf) bulbs which flower before most herbaceous plants are in active growth and which can therefore be used in extensive drifts throughout the planting, and those taller bulbs which flower in late spring, in summer and autumn and can be used in small groups to provide bright spots of colour in much the same way as herbaceous plants are used.

It should be noted at this point that I use the word 'bulb' in its widest sense to include any plant with a swollen or knobbly basal portion sold via bulb catalogues. The horticultural use of the word bulb is vague and I omit, for example, *Eremurus*, *Anthericum* and *Dierama* which are best purchased as herbaceous plants (but include snowdrop, a true bulb, which is also more successfully transplanted without drying). Dahlias and begonias are also excluded, although they are sold by bulb merchants and have clearly recogniz-

able dried storage organs, because they need to be lifted annually and given treatment appropriate to tender perennials, under which heading they are included.

Early dwarf bulbs are innumerable but not all are suited to the use I have in mind, namely the carpeting of the flowery mead with a coloured tapestry of flowers before being swamped by the herbaceous plants which are to provide the next wave of flowers. Many beautiful crocus, for example, are quite unsuitable. Indeed, apart from very exceptional situations, they are not suited to open garden use at all, requiring a severe summer baking to ripen their corms. They are much better planted in special frames and regarded as exceedingly beautiful botanical specimens rather than as garden plants. *Crocus* there are, however, which revel in less arid situations. *C. tommasinianus* is the easiest and one of the best. Varying from almost white to purple but usually a pale lavender it flowers in February, opening almost flat on warm days, and multiplies freely. *C. chrysanthus* is, if anything, more beautiful. It looks delicate and at work we grew it initially in scree conditions where it grew well but it, too, escapes its alloted space and is now growing very successfully among hellebores, under shrubs and even (though not very productively) in the same shade that makes our *Sarcococca* so elegant. At home a small and forgotten group emerged quite unscathed when its blanket of *Ajuga* and *Hebe* was brought under control and I am now convinced that it is a good plant for use for the coloured carpet here under consideration, especially good as it must be the most variable *Crocus* species varying from the creamy white of 'Snowbunting' and pale yellow of 'E.A. Bowles' to the smartly tailored purple and white suit of 'Ladykiller'.

The hybrid Dutch crocus are very different in character. Whereas, one marvels that the slender species can weather the winter storms the Dutch crocus are obviously built for the task: robust, healthy and round-cheeked they are among the brightest early flowers and tolerate a wide range of soils and situations. Many people dismiss them as gross: I like them but it must be repeated that they are very different from the species and that both hybrids and species suffer when grown together, each emphasizing the qualities of the other to the extent that qualities become faults. Two other points need to be borne in mind when using crocus informally. Firstly the yellow hybrids are sterile. The purple and white ones will increase steadily by

offsets and by seed gradually spreading to form large drifts. The yellows increase readily by offsets but remain as tight clumps which look more and more out of place in a mixture. It is better, therefore, either to avoid mixing the two colour ranges in the first instance (the range from white to purple is quite sufficient in itself) or, if a mixture must be had, to use *C. aureus* or *C. susianus* to provide fertile yellow flowers. The second point also involves colour comparisons. The colours of crocus (species and Dutch hybrids) are often strong and always warm. They do not associate at all well with many other flowers of that season. The yellows are especially bad with the more papery texture and acid yellows of early daffodils, winter aconites and even winter jasmine. The white Dutch crocus make snowdrops and Christmas roses look as dingy as the shirts washed in the other detergent in a soap advertisement. Purple crocus look dreadful with many blue flowers including the common grape hyacinths *Muscari*, *Omphalodes verna* and forget-me-nots *Myosotis*. It is easy to overstate the problem: winter aconites, crocus and daffodils tend to meet only in passing because of different flowering times; in any extensive areas of spring bulbs and associated plants the colour clashes seem to fade under constant repitition and to become insignificant in the general gaiety. In very small gardens, however, where individual clumps of bulbs assume more significance, it is worth the effort of resolving such clashes. One intractable problem in our garden results from the continuing population of forget-me-nots which contains a moderate proportion of pink-flowered plants. Blue forget-me-nots do not associate well with purple crocus; pink forget-me-nots blend beautifully with them, and with *Pulmonaria* but look awful with primroses, yellow crocus and aconites. As there is no way of knowing which forget-me-nots will be pink or blue until the flowers open we welcome the flowers, tolerate the clashes and weed vigorously before taking any photographs.

There are many other early bulbs suitable for interplanting with herbaceous plants or underplanting beneath deciduous shrubs. *Chionodoxa luciliae* and *Scilla sibirica* have blue flowers, very pale in chionodoxa, deeper in scilla. All increase by seed, they intercross to some extent and produce a range of flowers in all shades of blue. *Eranthis*, the winter aconite has already been mentioned as an acid-yellow flower. *E. hyemalis* is the smallest of the three commonly grown but small size is no disadvantage for early flowers and as it is robust, spreads freely by rhizomes and seeds, and has a smart green frill around each flower it is a very good plant. It also disappears completely by late April, a very useful habit in mixed plantings. Snowdrop *Galanthus* foliage is much longer lived but established groups of snowdrop do not appear to suffer if the leaves are swamped by other foliage before they have died away. There is no more beautiful early flower than the

snowdrop and although I appreciate the additional stature of *G. elwesii* and other large flowered forms, and can even be interested by the neat green rosettes in the centre of double-flowered forms, the ordinary *G. nivalis* still

remains at the top of the list. As the snowdrops have a very short dormant period and are damaged by dry storage it is better to obtain clumps of established bulbs in growth than dry bulbs. This is especially so if the clumps can be obtained from friends, for I am astonished at the price now asked for a single tiny snowdrop bulb. If suitable friends are not available it is more economical to obtain dry bulbs – as early in the autumn as one possible can – unless one is interested in the very rare and expensive forms of which losses cannot be contemplated. Snowdrops thrive in moist positions and are therefore easily kept away from any crocus which might impair the greenish white beauty of flower.

Of the iris, *I. reticulata* must be men-

Snowdrops grow in moist places and will tolerate submergence among hostas etc

tioned as an early-flowering dwarf for sunny, well drained positions. It is not only bright, robust and elegant (these two adjectives are not incompatible in iris) but fascinating to watch as the flower buds open very rapidly in warmth. Anyone having an opportunity to spend an hour or so working in the vicinity of its opening flowers will also discern another attribute, for *I. reticulata* is pleasantly scented. Like many early bulbs its leaves grow mainly after flowering and can become embarrassingly long and untidy but are made less so by immersing in other plants. This iris is a bulb for sunny, well drained situations so total immersion in a dense vegetable blanket will soon cause its demise but plants up to 15 cm (6 in) or so in height will adequately support and conceal the long iris leaves. *Linaria purpurea* and *Aquilegia* have leaves which unfurl at just the right time and of just the right glaucous green, and we have a *Euphorbia*, the name of which we have not yet ascertained, which is ideal in synchronizing its appearance with the departure of *Iris reticulata*. Their teamwork is further described in Chapter 18.

Ipheion uniflorum has had a chequered taxonomic career, being known as *Brodiaea uniflorum*, *Triteleia uniflorum* and *Ipheion*. It shares with the easier grape hyacinths (*Muscari armeniacum*, *M. racemosum*) a rapid rate of increase and unfortunate leaves but requires different treatment to combat the problem. *Ipheion* is a low plant, the very pale blue star like flowers being on stems

7 cm (3 in) tall, and it requires an open sunny situation. It will not tolerate prolonged smothering and is best grown in marginal groups among darker green plants to be followed by annuals or tender perennials so that the tangled mat of leaves has a chance to ripen before its blanket becomes too dense. *Muscari*, on the other hand, will survive any maltreatment. In one garden with a long history of grape hyacinth invasion the owner has developed an intense dislike of the plant and regularly wages warfare with a variety of potent herbicides. The bulbs increase less rapidly, but otherwise appear unabashed. The flowers of grape hyacinth are beautiful and borne in great profusion in April, after most of the other low bulbs, but the leaves begin to appear in late autumn, continue to grow through the winter and by April–May present an unruly mat of undistinguished bright green leaves which persist for longer than is respectable. The answer here is to grow the bulbs in broad drifts through the centre of the flowery mead, for the flowers are beautiful, but do ensure that the leaves are rapidly smothered by all the herbaceous plants that can be mustered for the attack. The *Muscari* will survive such treatment indefinitely.

With the one exception of *Eranthis* all the low bulbs thus far listed are genuinely bulbous or cormous and belong to the respectable families of bulbs (*Liliaceae* etc.). To accompany *Eranthis*, both in the book and in the garden, the early anemones are ideal.

Like *Eranthis* the anemones are members of the *Ranunculaceae*, the buttercup family, and have slowly spreading rhizomes which, in some instances, are sufficiently knobbly to be broken into short rounded tubers. The florists' anemone is not suited to prolonged garden use but *Anemone blanda* and *A. appenina* most certainly are. Both are basically blue but with white, pink and more double flowered forms. *A. appenina* is probably the most generally useful plant producing its feathery leaves early in the year, flowering in March–April then rapidly fading away so that it can be grown under trees, maturing before the leafy canopy emerges, and of course ideal for carpeting the flowery mead, preferably in the absence of purple crocus. I have also seen it in long grass. The flowers close and droop in rainy weather cleverly imitating a graceful *Soldanella* and in no way diminishing their beauty. *A. blanda* is a stockier and generally deeper coloured flower. In most gardens it requires a sunny, open situation when in flower but dies away sufficiently rapidly after flowering to tolerate immediate smothering. On well drained chalk soils, such as ours is to excess, it spreads freely even in shade, and the extensive carpets of *Anemone blanda* at Highdown, near Worthing, are something of a legend. It has a much longer flowering season than does *A. appenina*, from February to April, much of the long season being due to variation between plants. Our group is still sufficiently small to recognize the one plant crouching on the soil

surface in early February then leaping up to expand leaves and flowers on the first sunny day. Other plants follow in turn and it would be fun to develop colonies from these individuals and to plant them out in such a way that a sheet of *A. blanda* moved slowly round the garden. If only life were longer!

Another dicotyledonous (broad leaved) plant reminds us that a carpet of flowers can be had not only before leaves expand in the spring but after they have gone in the autumn. The hardy cyclamen are so dependable that I never cease to wonder that they are not more widely grown. Is it because the truly hardy species are listed amongst so many similar but marginally hardy or distinctly tender ones striking fear into the otherwise adventurous gardener? Is it because everyone has read of the confused nomenclature of *Cyclamen coum* and thinks that the plants will be as hard to grow as they are to name? I think it is because the plants are so exquisitely delicate in appearance that people consider they must have equally delicate constitutions. The purchase of large very dry corms of *C. hederifolium* (formerly *C. neapolitanum*) which seldom grow satisfactorily would confirm this suspicion. However, bought as small, actively growing potted seedlings, *Cyclamen hederifolium*, *C. purpurascens* (formerly *C. europaeum*), *C. coum* (or whatever else you choose to call it) and *C. repandum* are easily grown and usually increase steadily. All require some protection from the hurly-burly which is usually the keynote of the flowery mead and the best situation is at the very front of the planting with other very low plants, perhaps around the base of small trees where they can be both admired and protected from the onslaught of advancing geraniums or other taller plants. *C. hederifolium* is undoubtedly the easiest and one of the most useful, flowering in September and producing its beautifully marbled leaves soon after the flowers to form a close carpet which lasts through the winter and into the following summer. One could conceal the group from June onwards with a sowing of low hardy annuals – *Eschscholzia caespitosa* is ideal – to be pulled out before life begins anew in August and the late E. A. Bowles recommended interplanting with *Asarina procumbens* (*Antirrhinum asarina*) but a better reward for such sterling service would be a thin

With their elegant foliage the hardy cyclamen do not need to be submerged after flowering

mulch of leafmould. All cyclamen require good drainage but are not otherwise noted for fussiness as to soil type. Our *C. hederifolium* is successfully invading the margins of a gravel drive.

C. purpurascens flowers with or just before *C. neapolitanum* and is a smaller plant but with very sweetly scented flowers. It does well in lightly shaded situations and is nearly evergreen: *Cyclamen coum* is a small, neat plant, chubby is probably the best adjective for its bright purple-red flowers. Its leaves may lack the elegant marbling of other species but this is quite forgivable as *C. coum* flowers undaunted by weather in January. *C. repandum* is the least hardy of the four species and may need some shelter in the north of England. It is, however, a large flowered plant with attractively marbled foliage pro-

duced at the same time as the flowers, namely April or early May.

Other autumn flowering bulbs are the true autumn *Crocus*, *Colchicum* (often mistakenly called autumn crocus) and *Sternbergia Crocus speciosus* is the easiest autumn crocus with large pale lavender flowers. It will usually flower freely within weeks of being planted in August and then not be seen for a year or two. When settled in its new home it will usually flower freely and increase steadily to form large colonies. *Colchicum speciosum* superficially resembles a crocus but is not at all closely related. It, too, flowers in August–September but beware using it too freely as its leaves, produced in spring, are most un-crocus like vaguely resembling bright pea-green leeks or arums and sufficiently large to be embarrassing. *Sternbergia*

lutea also resembles a crocus but a large deep yellow one. This is a beautiful plant but unfortunately requires a hot summer for good development and will usually fade out gradually unless in an especially favourable garden. It is not expensive, however, and is worth introducing from time to time in the hope that it will settle down to a long and productive life. Both *Crocus* and *colchicum* will grow in thin grass and can therefore be relied upon to tolerate the less severe competition from low herbaceous or annual plants and do not therefore strictly need to follow after herbaceous foliage.

To return to later spring when herbaceous plants are rapidly coming into growth the use of bulbs has to be more restricted and, instead of carpeting the ground generally it is necessary

Colchicum 'The Giant'. Colchicums are striking flowers but are easily damaged by autumn gales. Their large leaves can be a problem in the spring garden

to leave spaces within the evergreen and herbaceous planting of sufficient size to accommodate bulbs. Bluebells, both the slender *Hyacinthoides non-scripta* and the more robust Spanish bluebell, *H. hispanica* are the last of the spring bulbs sufficiently robust to push their way through the rapidly developing carpet of herbaceous plants.

Tulips, most of which follow closely on the heels of the bluebells require a clearing in which to grow and this can be achieved either by leaving long thin gaps in the planting sufficient for two or three rows of closely spaced tulips or by leaving more extensive spaces in which broader groups can be used in a manner more similar to bedding. The brilliant colours of May flowering tulips are sufficiently strong that a series of thin drifts of bulbs through the planting is sufficient to produce a very pleasing effect, the individual flowers floating above the surrounding plants like poppies in a field instead of being lost in a tight blob of colour and the dying foliage of the tulips is not too conspicuous. When larger groups are used it is obviously necessary to make some use of the ground after the tulips have finished. This can be done either by removing the tulips and replacing them with summer bedding plants exactly as one might with more formal flower beds, or by sowing quick-growing hardy annuals or planting tender perennials or bulbs (*Gladiolus*, *Tigridia*) between the dying tulips. Left in position in this way the tulips are far more likely to increase than if they are disturbed

soon after flowering and the dying foliage is adequately camouflaged and eventually concealed by the summer planting.

Gladioli are difficult plants to use in the ornamental garden because of their very stiff nature but spread liberally in many small groups throughout the flowery mead, ideally following tulips, they are seen at their best. Unless the garden is exceptionally sheltered the large flowered hybrids require staking, a time consuming and difficult chore for *Gladiolus* but it is worth planting deeply and hoping to avoid staking for the sake of the bright spires of flowers in a range of colours as wide as that of the tulips. Although tulips can be left for several years in well drained soil, *Gladiolus* increases much more rapidly and unless the corms are lifted at least every other year they become congested with small corms, produce masses of leaves and very poor flowers. Although the flowers of *Gladiolus* are not long lived the foliage is a useful addition to a plant group and deadheading presents no problem. The season of flowering can be extended by selection of cultivars – most catalogues list early, mid and late flowering cultivars – and by successional planting of the corms at two week intervals.

Nerine bowdenii is better planted in association with early flowering bulbs than forced to compete with vigorous herbaceous plants. In this way the spring bulbs have ample room to display their beauty, and their foliage is beginning to die away by the time the

Nerine starts growing. The narrow, rather succulent leaves of *Nerine* are of good quality and provide a useful linear contrast to more rounded herbaceous forms. In late summer the foliage begins to die away, persisting longest on young non-flowering bulbs and from September to November a succession of beautiful pink flowers is produced, paying more than adequate rent for the ground occupied.

Lilies vary almost as much as all other bulbous plants put together, in height, in colour, in flower form and requirement of soil and situation. There is not room in this book to deal adequately with the genus *Lilium*, but it would be criminal not to mention lilies at least in passing and to remind readers that many are ideally suited to growing through thin undergrowth. Not everyone can grow the beautiful but demanding *Lilium auratum* to perfection but few would have trouble with *L. martagon* (1 m ≈ 4 ft; June–July), *L. hansonii* (1.5 m ≈ 5 ft; June–July), the beautifully scented *L. regale* (1.5 m ≈ 5 ft; July and one of the easiest to grow), the orange *L. davidii* (1.5 m ≈ 5 ft; August–September) or the taller *L. henryi* (up to 2 m ≈ 7 ft; also orange in August–September). *Lilium candidum*, the pure white Madonna lily, flowering in July is also easy where it will grow. It is one of the infuriating plants, like lily-of-the-valley *Convallaria*, stemless gentian

Lilium x *marhan* (*L. martagon* x *hansonii*) is one of the easiest lilies and grows well among other plants

123

Gentiana acaulis and Christmas rose *Helleborus niger* which have a reputation for growing with ease in one part of a garden while failing entirely in apparently similar situations elsewhere. On our thin, chalky soil Madonna lily bulbs sit on the soil surface, increase readily from bulb scales knocked off by passing rabbits and flower freely every year.

For colour later in the year the group of late summer flowering corms known variously as *Antholyza*, *Crocosmia*, *Curtonus*, *Montbretia* and *Tritonia* are particularly useful. I have always been confused by their naming but, as I now understand the situation (and my understanding is probably far from perfect) the plant with rapidly increasing masses of smooth light-green leaves and relatively small (45 cm ≈ 18 in) spikes of brownish orange flowers which I have always called 'montbretia' is really *Crocosmia x crocosmiiflora*. *Crocosmia mas-*

Crocosmia masonorum has bold, sword-shaped leaves and bright orange spikes in late summer

Opposite: Early bulbs can later be covered by herbaceous plants

oniorum has broadly pleated leaves looking very much like a seedling date palm and much branched spikes of reddish-orange flowers which twist on the stem to face upwards. *Antholyza paniculata* and *Curtonus paniculatus* are two names for one plant, the latter name being correct, and this plant has its flowers more widely spaced than *Crocosmia* on a distinctly zig-zagged stem up to a metre ($3\frac{1}{2}$ ft) tall. All other members of the five genera listed are very much inferior for garden use, being either less attractive or very much less hardy and more suited to cultivation in pots. The three mentioned are very good for their late summer flowers and also for their distinctive leaves. *Crocosmia* x *crocosmiiflora* ('montbretia') flowers much more freely when frequently divided but our plants have been left for four years to produce extensive and attractive grassy clumps and still produce abundant flowers. *Crocosmia masoniorum* I prefer to see frequently divided as small groups display the graceful arching habit so much better than do large clumps.

I have mentioned frequently the value of linear foliage for preventing a large planting of rounded plants becoming amorphous and uninteresting and *Crocosmias* and *Curtonus* are as useful in this respect as for their flowers. There are five other denizens of bulb catalogues which can be added to the list, summer snowflake *Leucojum aestivum*, St. Bruno's lily *Paradisea liliastrum*, wandflower or angels' fishing rods *Dierama pulcherrimum*, the hardy

hybrid *Agapanthus* and kaffir lily *Schizostylis coccinea*.

Leucojum aestivum is called summer snowflake because it flowers rather later in the spring than does the dwarfer spring snowflake *L. vernum*. It is, however, definitely spring flowering. As with the other four it would be an exaggeration to call summer snowflake a foliage plant but the leaves are borne in sturdy dark green clumps like exceptionally vigorous bluebells, an excellent foil to the small white flowers. They emerge early in the year and persist well into the summer. This is a true bulb and although naturally a waterside plant (also known as Loddon lily) it grows

Leucojum aestivum has strong leaves which persist long after the pendant white bells

Opposite: Herbaceous plants. *Hemerocallis* 'North Star' and forms of *Campanula lactiflora* at Shinfield Grange

127

Dierama pulcherrima: 'pulcherrima' means very beautiful. The leaves are an additional asset but eventually become bedraggled

freely in the driest parts of our very dry garden and must be counted extraordinarily adaptable.

Anthericum liliago is as pale and graceful as Leucojum is dark and sturdy. The flowers are borne on slender spikes in June, star-like with protruding anthers, and the foliage eventually forms thick clumps of pale green, the leaves often folding half way along their length to bend gracefully to the ground. *Dierama pulcherrimum* is aptly named angels' fishing rods. It is one of the most beautiful flowers with long arching stems weighed down by pendant pink flowers waving gracefully in the breeze. It is grown, of course, for its flowers but the leaves, although coarse and wiry, can be a decided asset in the flowery mead forming a fountain at the edge of the path. Although a tall plant, up to 1.5 m (5 ft) tall, at the edge of the path it must be to display its beautiful fishing rods to greatest advantage. *Agapanthus* and *Schizostylis* are later flowering but their leaves are produced in late spring and continue in excellent condition until after flowering. *Agapanthus* has fans of rather stiffly arching bright green leaves with the flowers borne in nearly spherical heads on slender stems well above the foliage. Flower colour varies from white to very dark blue, my preference being for the latter. Although one can do very well by purchasing unnamed Headbourne hybrids there are now many named cultivars and as some flower very much

White agapanthus, white Japanese anemone and yew hedges in September. Tintinhull

earlier than others – the season extending from August into October – it is often worth the additional expense in buying named cultivars to extend the flowering season to the full or to select the earlier flowering ones if the garden is already well endowed with autumn flowers. *Schizostylis coccinea* has thinner more upright leaves of pale glaucous green spreading by short rhizomes to form large colonies. The flowers, resembling very slender gladioli, are borne from October until the severest weather of November/December puts an end to the display. Selected colour forms vary from pink to scarlet. Thick clumps tend to look rather untidy and flowering is greatly improved by dividing and replanting such clumps.

For situation, *Leucojum* is supposed to grow in very wet soils but obviously does not realize this in our garden. *Anthericum* and *Dierama* require adequate moisture: the latter will grow successfully at the waterside and on heavy clay. *Schizostylis* requires a warm situation but not necessarily a dry one: one of our groups grows very well in a shaded border but with warmth from the house wall. *Agapanthus* is a plant for sunny and well drained, even dry, situations. Although all five are frequently listed in bulb catalogues only the snowflake is a true bulb. The others are fleshy rooted or vaguely cormous and better bought with the roots moist and intact as herbaceous plants, which brings me to herbaceous plants.

129

Chapter **15**

Herbaceous Perennials

ALTHOUGH the bulbs are perhaps most efficient at insinuating their bright colours into the limited space of a garden, herbaceous plants provide a good display of flowers as well as clothing the ground in attractively coloured and textured foliage. Again it has been necessary to be very selective to fit the list of plants into the available pages and again selection has not been on the basis of a plant's rarity but on good garden value, on plants which contribute to the garden for the longest possible period and are seldom unsightly.

The mainstays of the flowery mead are the middle-height rounded plants. *Brunnera macrophylla* and *Anemone hupehensis* var. *japonica* were mentioned with other good plants in Chapter 2 but deserve a second mention as very early and very late flowering plants respectively. The euphorbias also flower early. *Euphorbia wulfenii* usually begins in April and like so many euphorbias continues more or less indefinitely, the flowers paling but losing none of their interest in several months. Quite by

contrast the paeony season is measured in days instead of months but the flowers are *so* beautiful and the foliage is of considerable value. Although paeony foliage is quite large it heralds a group of plants with similar quality of foliage, generally palmately divided or lobed in bright or blue green, which mingle very well together. *Dicentra* and *Corydalis* follow close on the heels of paeonies in flowering season but are much smaller and more fragile looking. *Dicentra spectabilis* is fleeting in flower and, on our light soil, of fleeting existence but *D. eximea* and especially *D. e.* 'Alba' seem to tolerate any situation and to flower sporadically for much of the summer. *Corydalis lutea* is even more obliging: its much divided pale grey-green leaves and translucent stems give the plant a very frail appearance which it belies by growing freely in any soil, in chinks in the paving, in old brick walls and other hostile situations. It, too, begins to flower in May but continues – to say 'sporadically' is to greatly under-estimate the plant's efforts – often into the autumn. Midsummer, July and

August, is not a period noted for abundance of flowers but *Astrantia major* is then at its best. The flowers are not spectacular but have a neat, rather charming appearance with a pincushion centre surrounded by papery bracts of 'whitish-pinkish-lavender'. The leaves are deeply lobed and associate well with the other plants mentioned above as do the leaves of *Astilbe*. Although at their best in very moist soils astilbes will survive in drier soils and make thick, weed-free clumps of very dark green foliage, with their feathery panicles of flower also appearing in July and August. The hellebores close and open the season by flowering principally from December to March. *Helleborus foetidus* receives rave-reviews elsewhere in the book but mention should also be made of the paler, broader leaves of *H. argutifolius*, the lower-growing *H. niger* and the later-flowering *H. orientalis* bringing the flowering season of these dissected-leaved plants round again to paeony time.

In complete contrast the genus *Hosta* provides a foliar undividedness of great quality as well as late summer flowers. These are mentioned in Chapter 7. The border *Phlox* flower unstintingly and in a range of brilliant colours in the deadest part of the late summer season. Their foliage is not outstanding (except in being produced commendably early in the spring) unless of course one grows the variegated 'Harlequin' but neither is it unsightly. Removal of the flower heads when they have finished will often result in a second flush of smaller

Hosta sieboldiana . . . a masterpiece of foliar undividedness

inflorescences. Unlike most of the plants mentioned in this section, *Phlox* is much better if divided frequently but will certainly tolerate neglect in this respect. It is pointless to recommend cultivars from the enormous range offered – go to a good catalogue and select the colour and height required – but I must just mention 'Mia Ruys'. Although *Phlox* is eminently better on moist soils, the white flowered 'Mia Ruys' has grown vigorously for several years on our very light soil. If divided frequently it is a useful dwarf among the border *Phlox*, about 50 cm (18 in) tall but after two or three years in the same position will nearly double that height.

The old *Tradescantia virginiana* earned its name 'Moses in the bullrushes' by carrying its not over-conspicuous dark blue flowers even less conspicuously down among the leaves. The newer hybrids such as 'Bluestone' have lost none of the good linear foliage of the species but have larger flowers displayed rather more conspicuously on compact plants. They begin to flower in July but continue more or less indefinitely thereafter.

Two good plants to close the season are *Aster acris* 'Nana' and *Anaphalis nubigena*. Many of the lower growing Michaelmas daisies are bright and compact but so often succumb to mildew or mites which ruin the foliage and flowers respectively. I grow one especially bright purple but am always more satisfied by the performance of *Aster acris* 'Nana', a dome of fine-textured light green all summer buried under hundreds of small spiky narrow-rayed mauve flowers in autumn. Like the *Phlox* 'Mia Ruys', this plant needs frequent division (preferably every year) to keep it below 40 cm (15 in) and if allowed to grow taller always disgraces itself by falling apart to display a circle of sticks. *Anaphalis nubigena* is another low plant, rather wider spreading than the aster, but with grey foliage and white everlasting flowers which remain in good condition for the autumn and much of the winter. There are taller members of this genus. *A. triplinervis* being up to 75 cm ($2\frac{1}{2}$ ft) tall but the compact shape and distinct foliage of *A. nubigena* remind me very much of a dwarf grey *Viburnum davidii* – praise indeed!

Aster acris 'Nana', more interesting than the heavier Michaelmas daisies especially in the many months before flowering

The herbaceous members of the genus *Geranium* (as distinct from the garden geraniums which are properly *Pelargonium*) are currently as popular as they arc varied and they deserve their popularity. Some, such as *G. renardii* with its thick felty olive green leaves and *G. wlassovianum*, again with good foliage and bright, two-tone flowers are fairly compact. The latter is not widely grown, perhaps because of its tongue-twisting name, but is to be recommended for the splendid autumn tints of its foliage. Others are more stemmy and spread more widely by leafy stolons to cover a large area. The low, pink flowered *G. endressii* 'Wargrave Pink' and the taller *G.* 'Johnson's Blue' are moderate spreaders and will insinuate themselves between more compact plants in a reasonably gentle manner. When low plants are threatened the geraniums are easily restrained by pulling off the offending branch but, allowed to wander among taller plants, the geraniums are ideal for unifying the planting.

Anthemis cupaniana travels similarly but more woodily and has an extra-ordinarily long flowering season. It is really an evergreen (or ever-grey) but benefits by having herbaceousness (herbaceocity?) forced upon it by cutting hard back in spring or whenever it spreads beyond bounds. Only once have I seen a good clump of *Oenothera missouriensis* and although *O. acaulis* (*O. taraxacifolia*) is rather better behaved it, too, has distinctly straggling tendencies which are best accommodated by planting in the flowery mead and allowing the evening primroses to peep out where they will. The first example I had of this was when a patch of *Phlox subulata* suddenly sprouted large white flowers in late summer. *Oenothera acaulis* will often root at the nodes forming a loose carpet in the same manner as another straggler, *Potentilla astrosanguinea*. This bright-red flowered plant is too loose for grouping in the herbaceous border but is ideally at home in the flowery mead. Violas are of similar habit: one can cut them back to form neat mounds but left to wander they will flower over a long period. *Viola cornuta* is, unfortunately, suited only to moist soils but we grow the lower, purple leaved *V. labradorica* satisfactorily and the native heartsease (*V. tricolor*) is at home even in thin grass.

For the edge of a planting a good proportion of evergreen plants is desirable and *Alyssum*, *Aubrieta*, *Iberis*, and *Helianthemum* receive due consideration elsewhere. A continuous band of evergreens along a border in which herbaceous plants have left large gaps in the winter is not desirable so many low herbaceous plants find a place. *Ajuga reptans* is almost evergreen and inhabits many a damp lawn but the purple leaved form is very desirable. It spreads rapidly but hugs the ground and will usually run beneath rather than over other plants. The rich blue flowers are borne on spikes well above the foliage and can be sheared off when finished. *Tiarella cordifolia* is similar –

133

but different. It, too, spreads close to
the ground, is usually evergreen or
nearly so but has very light green leaves
and masses of delicate white flowers
amply justifying its common name of
'foam flower'. *Epimedium* and *Ceratostigma* are other non-identical twins.
Both spread (much more slowly than
Ajuga and *Tiarella*) by underground
stems and seem to survive among the
roots of trees and in other hostile
situations. *Epimedium* is at its best
early in the year when the graceful
flowers are closely followed by bronzy
young foliage expanding to pale, often
almost translucent, green. The leaves
persist into the winter and are attractive
even in their dry state but are best removed in late winter to display the
flowers which would otherwise remain
concealed. *Ceratostigina plumbaginoides*
is slow to emerge from the winter but
gradually thickens into a good cushion.
Just as one thinks it has forgotten about
flowering the bright blue flowers appear at the tips of each shoot in October/
November and simultaneously the
leaves begin to turn purple or crimson
to set the little flowers off to perfection.

Shasta daisy *Chrysanthemum maximum*
is not the first plant to spring to mind as
an edger but its close relative *Leucanthemum* 'Little Silver Princess' is excellent
for this purpose. The rosettes of very
dark green leaves extend in mid-summer to produce dozens of yellow-
centred white daisies on stems up to
25 cm (9 ins) tall. This is a new plant
with me and may well be another requiring frequent division to keep it low.

134

After flowering the dead stems are easily cut away leaving a 5 cm (2 in) mat of dark green for the autumn. This year has produced rather exceptional weather (don't they all!) and my 'Little Silver Princess' is flowering prolifically in December after some autumn flowering so perhaps it should also be included in the winter garden!

Limonium latifolium, sea lavender, is also flowering in December but has obviously read the text books and usually flowers in July. Like most plants suited especially to hot, dry positions (it grows also elsewhere) it is best left alone after planting. For two years after lifting and dividing to increase my meagre stock the plants were very unproductive but they have now settled to produce good groups. The leaves are like long bright green tongues, not as large as *Bergenia* but making a good bold group. The inflorescence, in contrast, is a slender much branched head of tiny pale lavender flowers which can be dried for winter decoration. The stem is not firmly anchored to the tuft of leaves and often topples unless given a short stake but this is not a disaster. One nice feature of *Limonium* is that you can give it away and keep it: it grows from root cuttings and if the plant is dug up the root fragments left in the soil will regenerate new plants. This is especially worth remembering as, after a few years the plants become disfigured by retaining old, dead leaves. If there is not time to sort out the new from the old one can simply hoe off the top (which

Tiarella cordifolia, aptly named foam-flower, is almost evergreen and forms attractive colonies. The foliage turns foxy red in winter

135

with care can be divided and rooted to form a new colony) and leave the plant to form fresh new leaves.

Pulmonaria is useful for its early spring flowers and for the spotted green leaves which thereafter ensue, while at the other end of the garden calendar *Sedum spectabile* forms fat cushions of fleshy grey leaves with flat plates of pink flowers in the autumn. It is an impeccable plant in the worst of weather but usually manages to flower in the October sunshine when it is smothered by butterflies. Frost reduces the leaves to a mush but the rosy brown seed heads remain decorative for months.

One effect which I find especially attractive is the use of plants with low foliage and much taller slender flowers. The plants themselves are varied, as the short list below indicates but long drifts of such plants, not necessarily deep drifts, create beautiful scenes by the repeated emphasis of many vertical lines. At the bottom of the scale *Ajuga reptans* and *Tiarella cordifolia* have already been mentioned. Taller and much later are the elegant spires of *Physostegia virginiana*, its white-flowered cultivar 'Summer Snow' and the fuzzy purple feathers of *Liatris spicata*, unusual in opening from the top of the spike downwards. *Kniphofia* and *Sidalcea* share a common habit of producing vertical spires on young plants but as each crown grows the stems, including flower stems fan out at an increasing angle from the vertical. *Kniphofia* plants often correct themselves and the stems

curve but *Sidalcea* I divide frequently to keep the youthful habit of slender vertical stems adorned with pale pink mallow-like flowers. A similar treatment is accorded to *Iris sibirica*, a supposed water-side plant which grows very well on our dry soil. In time it produces enormous clumps, prolific in flower but swamping any nearby plants in a very ungainly and unfriendly fashion. Dividing therefore benefits the iris and its neighbours. Like the iris, *Aquilegia* (columbine) has not spikes of flower but long stems with a small group of flowers at the top. Nevertheless the predominant effect is of vertical lines. The same applies – as does almost every other flattering remark made in this book – to the much longer lived Japanese anemone, *A. hybrida*.

The king of vertical spires must be the delphinium, in every shade of blue and purple with some good cream cultivars and one or two verging on pink. Delphiniums are hard work – they must be thinned, staked, sprayed, periodically renewed – but they are beautiful. More difficult even than the work involved is their propensity for leaving tattered remains across embarrassingly large areas of ground when the June flowering season is over. One might cut the plants back and sow quick-growing annuals, or cover the skeletons with climbers for later colour. I avoid tall delphiniums partly because of the engineering problems in keeping them upright but also, of necessity, because tall delphiniums do not grow tall on our soil without more care and attention than I am able to give. However the form and colour of delphinium is such that I could not do without some medium growing ones – 1.5 m (5 ft or so) tall which we have in long thin groups interplanted with plume poppy, *Macleaya cordata*. The latter does not grow rapidly in the early part of the year and by delphinium-flowering time is just over half metre (nearly 2 ft) high with large grey leaves with brilliant white reverses, splendid for flower arranging. As delphiniums wane the *Macleaya* waxes, producing its 2 m (6 ft) spires of tiny flowers in August to conceal the wreckage of the delphiniums while not completely smothering their new growth.

One last herbaceous plant fitting into none of the categories thus far dealt with is the oriental poppy, *Papaver orientale*. It is beautiful, it is brilliant with its huge orange or red flimsy petalled flowers (pinkish white in 'Pely's White') but my goodness it looks dreadful in late May when it has finished flowering. Fortunately it grows from root cuttings and the whole plant can be chopped off to regenerate later. We grow it mingled – as you might guess – with Japanese anemone which very nicely takes over where the poppy left off. After its midsummer rest the poppy starts into growth in autumn and produces foliage which can brighten winter and early spring.

Chapter 16

Annuals and Tender Perennials

HARDY shrubs, bulbs and herbaceous perennials have had to adapt to marked seasonal changes and usually flower profusely but for a short season to allow the other important activities of growing, setting seed and preparing for winter to take place in good time. Shrubs and herbaceous plants can be chosen to extend the season of interest by providing pleasing foliage or contrasts in form but for flowers the most unstinting plants are those which can literally flower themselves to death with no more provision for the future than a scattering of seed – the annuals – and those which evolved without the need to cater for inclement seasons – the tropical and subtropical shrubs such as *Pelargonium* (confusingly known as 'geranium'). Many provide a long season of colour to enliven the flowery mead.

Many of the plants here described are commonly known as bedding plants but, as William Robinson spared no pains to point out, bedding itself is not advisable in small gardens and is of

limited value in large gardens. Where the pattern of flower beds is itself pleasing and no further winter interest is necessary, then formal bedding is an acceptable and very colourful technique but good bedding requires a lot of work and a uniform area. In small gardens the inevitable proximity of buildings results in variations of shade, rainfall, temperature so the plants develop unevenly. The only suitable place would be in the open centre of the garden, and in small gardens more than anywhere else it is vitally important to leave the centre open and uncluttered. However, to throw the bedding plants out with formal bedding is to throw the baby out with the bathwater as many adapt well to the flowery mead.

Of the spring flowering plants forget-me-not *Myosotis*, *Aubrieta*, polyanthus and wallflower *Cheiranthus cheiri* must be mentioned. Forget-me-not is a very trouble free plant. If, after flowering, one or two of the best plants are left to ripen seed and then shaken vigorously over the area to be covered, thick colonies of seedlings arise. These are easily removed where unwanted and elsewhere thinned to a few inches apart, quickly carpeting the ground to form a sheet of blue flowers in the spring. As soon as the flowers start to fade the plants are easily pulled up, leaving just a few as before. It is wise not to delay the clearance for too long as forget-me-not, small though the plants seem in the autumn, can expand to cover a surprising amount of ground in their flowering season and can surreptitiously swamp newly emerging plants. *Aubrieta* is a more permanent plant and can be used as part of the evergreen margin to a border. Named cultivars can be obtained but a packet of mixed seed gives a surprising range of early and late, compact and spreading plants in many shades of red, purple and pink. It is a simple matter to increase desirable plants by cuttings of new growth taken after flowering and shearing plants will keep them compact and extend their useful life. If required

as a temporary inhabitant, *Aubrieta* can be cut right back, pulled apart and lined out in a nursery until the autumn, but it is such an attractive plant in leaf that such treatment is a waste of effort. Polyanthus can be semi-permanent. Although perennials, their leaves have not the attraction of *Aubrieta* and it may seem advisable to remove plants to the nursery after flowering. In small gardens a nursery is usually not available and as polyanthus tolerates very dense shading in the summer it is quite in order to leave them in position and simply grow other plants over them. Eventually plants become congested and sparse flowering so division every two or three years is advisable. Grown in this way the great number of small flowers resulting are much more appropriate to the flowery mead than are the huge but far fewer flowers of one year old plants grown for bedding. Wallflowers are grown not only for the colour of their flowers but for their

Cheiranthus 'Harpur Crewe', the perfume of a wallflower on bright evergreen hummocks

superb scent. They are quite useless in their second flowering season and must be scrapped after flowering, to be replaced by seed sown in June or July to produce plants for autumn planting. When space is not available for raising plants they can be purchased much more cheaply than other spring bedding plants, but if yellow flowers are appropriate to the garden then a much more delightful solution is to grow the very old perennial wallflower *Cheiranthus* 'Harpur Crewe'. This forms a neat dome of bright green leaves topped in spring with long-lasting small double flowers of bright yellow. The scent is everything a wallflower scent should be. Although it will eventually grow 45 cm (18 in) high and much more across it is much better when cut hard back after flowering to conserve its compact habit. Cut back or not it is not a long-lived perennial and will start to die back after four or five years but is very easily propagated by cuttings. One small flower pot will house enough cuttings to replace a good sized group of this delightful little wallflower.

Forget-me-nots can be relied on to find chinks between herbaceous plants to grow in the autumn and can be pulled up as the permanent occupants start into growth in the following spring. *Aubrieta* is a more permanent edging plant but the ground left vacant by wallflowers, polyanthus, spring bulbs and oriental poppies can be occupied in turn by summer annuals and tender perennials. These produce, in effect, seasonal but informal bedding schemes which do not rely on great numbers of uniform plants, nor leave great gaps in the small garden when not in flower.

Half-hardy annuals are most useful in such situations as they can be brought on under glass and transferred to the open garden in June by which time the earlier flowering plants have died away. Many of them have a long flowering season. For the edge of a planting *Felicia bergerana* is delightful, covered in little blue daisies all summer long and so productive that it can be lifted before frosts to continue as a dwarf pot-plant. *Cuphea ignea* is equally productive but less conspicuous with small scarlet flowers. Further back the tall antirrhinums make a splendid addition to the list of plants with vertical flower spikes. I prefer the old types of antirrhinum with closed flowers, deserving of the common names 'snapdragon' and 'bunny rabbit' and see no more reason in pentstemon-flowered types than in beef-flavoured lamb. However the seedsman must have his novelties to stimulate sales so I shall not complain loudly unless antirrhinum-flowered antirrhinums are considered so old-fashioned that they are omitted from seed lists: then some enterprizing breeder will be able to fill the gap with antirrhinum-flowered pentstemons no doubt. China aster (*Callistephus chinensis*) seems to me of limited value in the flowery mead. It is a splendid flower and if there is no other place to grow it then in the flowery mead it can go, but it does not flower until rather late in the season and its foliage in the meantime is undistinguished so I prefer to grow it in the vegetable garden for its long lasting cut flowers and to devote space in the ornamental garden to plants with a longer season of interest. The last of my short list of half-hardy annuals is *Nicotiana affinis*, the tobacco plant. This has been the subject of much improvement in recent years so beware: I grew a very attractive dwarf white last year – with no scent! The colour range is now extended and some strains open and are scented during the day as well as in the evening but if experimenting, be sure to buy only types which are stated in the catalogue to be strongly perfumed. Tobacco plant, although grown as an annual, is in fact a tender perennial and in milder parts of Britain will usually emerge in late spring from roots left in the soil after assigning tops to the bonfire or compost heap.

The most useful hardy annuals are those with a much shorter flowering season than the half-hardy annuals mentioned above. Whereas half-hardy annuals are planted out often on the point of flowering, hardy annuals have to undergo some vegetative growth before flowering and it seems such a waste to fill borders with undistinguished vegetation in anticipation of flowers some time in the autumn, probably to be ruined after a few weeks by frost. Those which flower most rapidly are, as one might expect, soon exhausted by the effort and look thoroughly disreputable by late summer. They are, however, ideal for

sowing after the oriental poppies and spring bulbs have finished to flower in July and August before dispatch to the compost heap in anticipation of the emergence of *Nerine bowdenii*, *Crocus speciosus* and *Colchicum*.

My favourite is *Eschscholzia caespitosa* (*E*. 'Miniature Primrose') the pale feathery foliage of which is attractive from the day it emerges. The sulphur yellow poppy-like flowers are borne in great profusion within six weeks of sowing and before the plants are pulled up they will have left a legacy of seeds to supply future generations. We have even had occasional plants appearing in quite tall grass under fruit trees. *Malcomia maritima* (Virginian stock) is a favourite children's plant so quickly does it flower. It is not a plant of substance and must be sown in rows quite close together to make a respectable carpet but is then spangled with small flowers of white, pink, red and purple all summer long. Another low but more spreading plant is *Ursinia anethoides*. I do not know if all varieties are equally obliging but the one we grow, 'Sunstar', does double duty as a flowering plant. The ray florets (for this is a member of *Compositae*) are bright sunny orange but when they fall they reveal shorter white florets to form quite a distinct and attractive second 'flower'. The habit of *Ursinia* is very similar to that of the *Eschscholzia* but the colour is much brighter. *Legousia speculum-veneris* Venus' looking glass is another attractive low carpet but with deep violet funnel-shaped flowers.

Two taller plants are *Mentzelia lindleyi* (*Bartonia aurea*) and *Nemophila insignis*. The former is deep yellow and makes a substantial mound if adequately thinned but thinning is yet one more task to break the gardener's back and – in times of stress – his spirit and the colony of a great many crowded plants with a few flowers on each is no less productive than a few widely spread plants with hundreds of flowers on each. I prefer, therefore, to sow all annuals thinly but in quite close rows, to thin the plants once just to avoid mass damping off, and then to let them grow as they will to produce a weed-smothering cover. This would not apply, of course to annuals with tall spikes of flowers which would be stunted by crowding, nor to those grown for cutting when vigorous growth and long stems are required but the 'all-over-sprinkle' flowering habit of the many annuals useful in the flowery mead is well suited to such treatment and *Nemophila insignis* with its multitude of little blue and white flowers requires the mutual support which such close spacing gives. Most of these annuals need to be grown in substantial groups to be effective. *Eschscholzia* is sufficiently conspicuous to be allowed to appear wherever it will, in cracks in paving or beneath and between any non-clashing plants. Another plant which I sprinkle about freely is love-in-a-mist *Nigella damascena* 'Miss Jekyll'. It is half naturalized in our garden and is always engaging

with its finely cut foliage, delicate blue flowers and puffed-up spiny-looking fruits. Being one of the very hardy annuals capable of growing through most English winters it is to be found in all stages of growth at any time of year and it is very seldom without flower.

Dahlias are of enormous value in the flower garden providing a wealth of rich colours and flower forms over a very long period from August to frost. Dahlia blurs the distinction between annuals and perennials because the single 'Coltness Gem' is usually grown from seed, preferably sown individually in small pots but boxes will do. Any especially good forms can be lifted and stored if required but as good forms seem to appear in every seed packet the effort is seldom justified. The taller and double-flowered named cultivars are grown as perennials and are better grown as tender perennials, lifting the tubers each autumn, starting them into growth early in the new year and rooting cuttings to form sturdy plants ready for their flowering positions in June. Dahlias are a matter of taste, some people would say bad taste. I enjoy the huge dinner-plates of flowers produced by pumping up the plants with enormous quantities of manure, water and fertilizer so long as they are in other people's gardens, I feel rather embarrassed for the 'ball' and 'pompom' dahlias with tiny globes of colour perched high on massive leafy bushes looking more ungainly than the most uncoordinated adolescent; I like and use the smaller decorative and cactus –

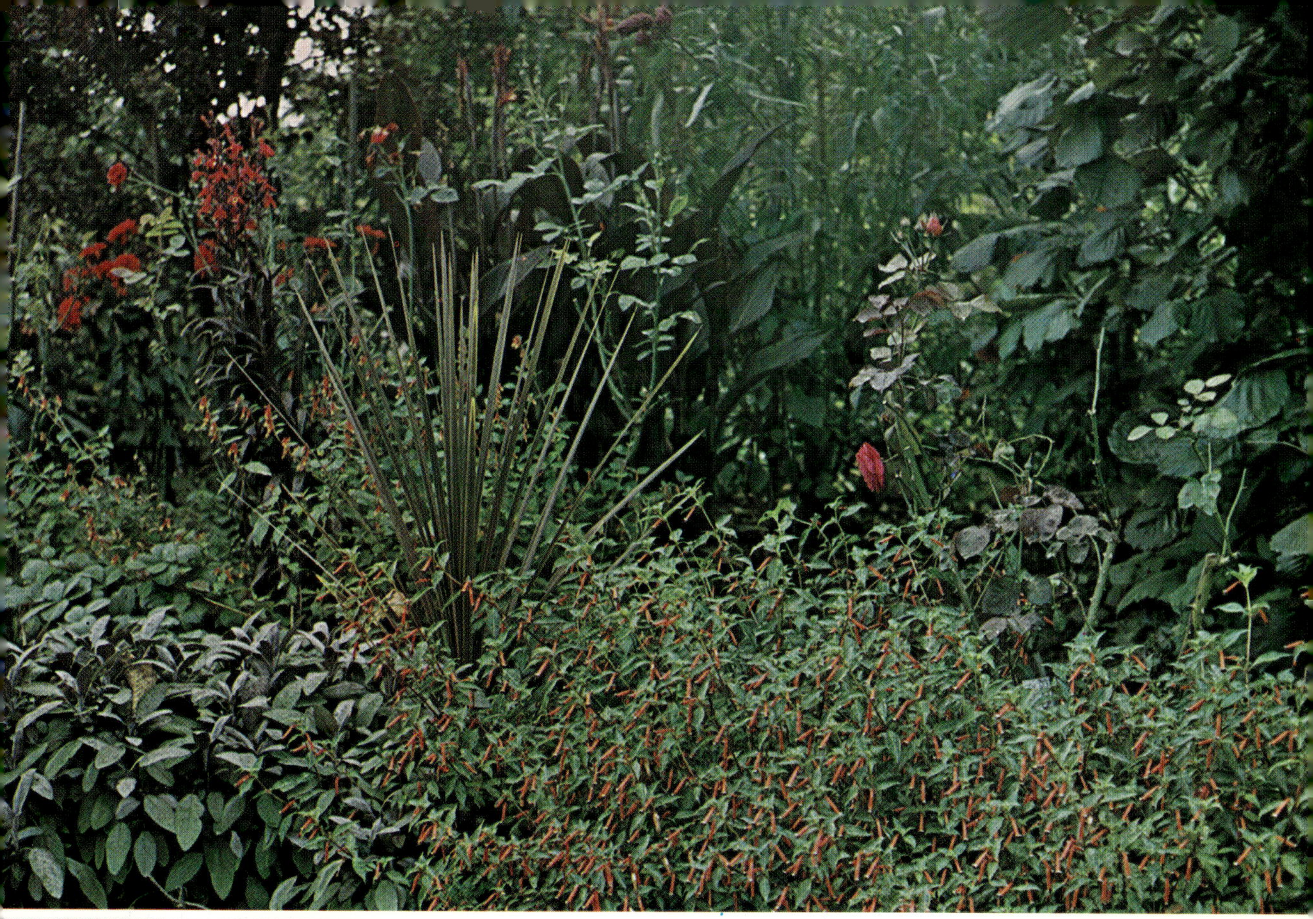

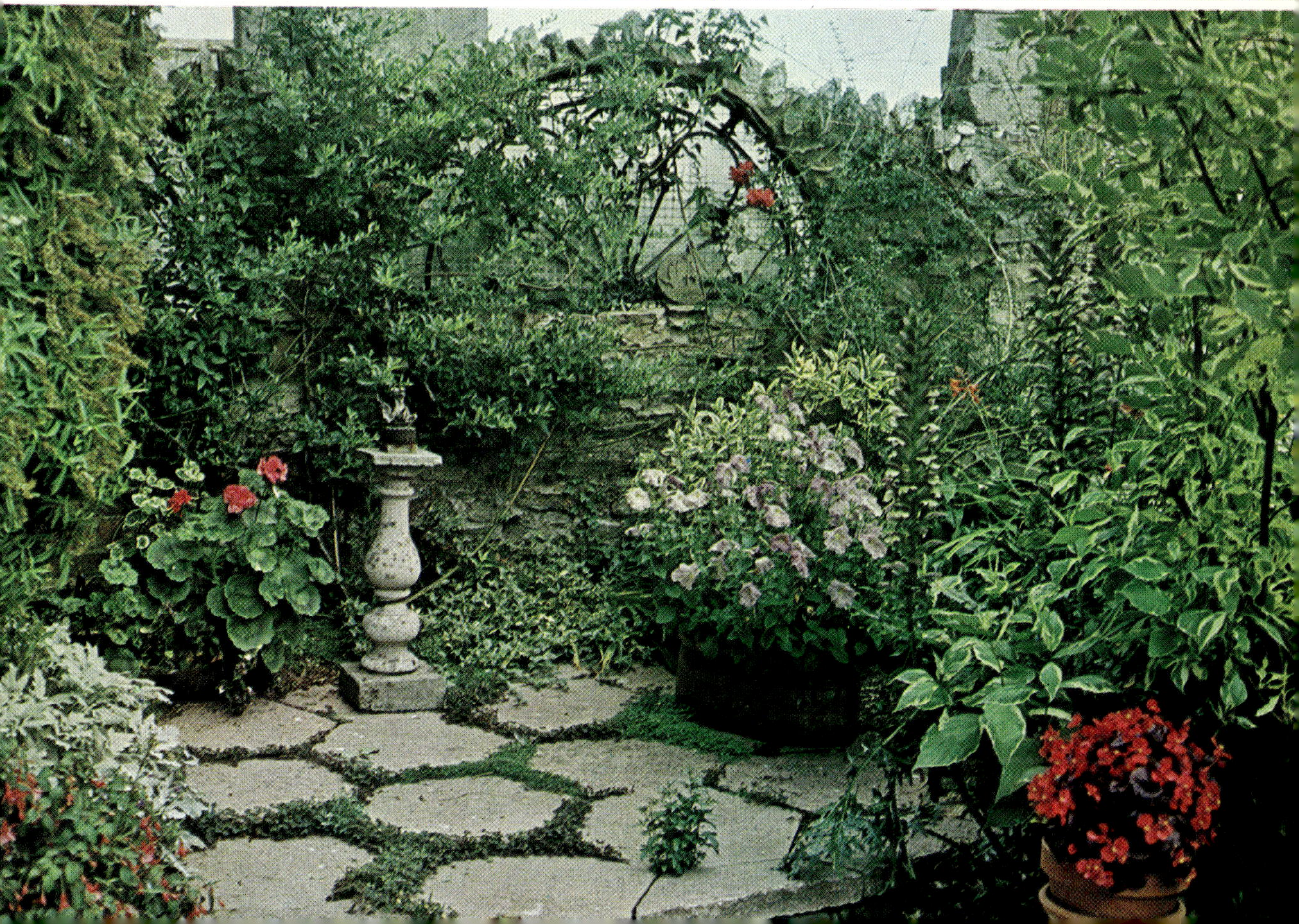

flowered cultivars and especially the neat-growing 'Park Princess', 'Border Princess' and 'Front Row'. Several of the reds have purple foliage inherited probably from the very old 'Bishop of Llandaff' and are thereby doubly attractive but there are so many cultivars to choose from that the best advice is to find the ones you like in friends' gardens and to beg cuttings!

Zonal *Pelargonium*, which most people insist on calling 'geraniums',

also suffer undeserved scorn. Scarlet, yellow and blue striped bedding may not be your idea of heavenly bliss (I think it amounts to masochism rather than bad taste) but there *are* other *Pelargonium* cultivars with flowers of white, pink, crimson and, my favourite, very soft orange. For every tiny gardens and in pots there are spiky-petalled *Pelargonium*, spiky leaved *Pelargonium*, coloured and scented leaved *Pelargonium* and more but for garden use

Opposite:
Wall plants and climbers. *Vitis coignetiae*, bold and brilliant

A fine mixed shrub and herbaceous border, relying heavily on contrasting foliage forms

the single smoothly rounded flowers are most admirable. Cuttings root easily in autumn or spring and can be planted out after frost for as long or as briefly as they are required to fill a gap, producing an unending succession of flowers borne clear of the foliage and lasting a long time in water.

Begonias, too, are worthy of mention. The fibrous rooted *Begonia semperflorens* is amazing. I have seen it growing at the base of privet hedges and in acres of sun-baked concrete, not only surviving but flowering prolifically. With flowers from white to deep red and leaves from pale green to deep purple/brown in all combinations the range is now enormous and this is a plant which can be planted out after frost to flower all summer long, pulled up and divided to make winter-flowering pot plants then divided again to make still bigger groups in the following year. The tuberous begonias with their succulent stems and enormous flowers are less easy and are quite fragile but can be used in a small jumbled one-of-every-thing cottage border. More manageable, however, are the smaller and much more floriferous intermediate begonias (hybrids between the fibrous and tuberous types).

Lastly on a more elegant note are the fuchsias. The enormous current popularity of fuchsias is hardly surprising. Few would contest that the pendant, long pistilled flowers are among the most elegant of flowers and, with the range from the small flowers of 'Mrs Lovell Swisher' to the enormous double 'Tennessee Waltz' this is truly a flower for all tastes. A surprising number of hybrid fuchsias are proving hardy, cut back perhaps by frost and then slow to break into growth and to produce flowers but perfectly good late summer flowering plants. *Fuchsia magellanica*, *F. m. molinae* (usually called *F. m. alba* despite its pink flowers) and *F. m.* 'Versicolor' with variegated leaves are quite hardy in most winters and eventually form large shrubs covered with flowers all summer and until the frosts. The fuchsia garden at Hidcote where low hardy fuchsias emerge as herbaceous perennials through a carpet of spring bulbs is a delightful example of the intermingling of plants to create a flowery mead of great simplicity and very long season of beauty.

Chapter 17

Wall Plants and Climbers

WALL plants and climbers are valuable additions to the range of plants available for small gardens. I use the phrase 'wall plants and climbers' rather than the usual title 'climbers and wall plants', which adorns the several good books on this subject, as a means of ensuring that we put the horse before the cart. To write first of climbers implies the necessity for some support and conjures visions of wire mesh being fastened all over the walls, constant pruning-back, tying-in and, in the case of the ever popular rose tribe, masochistic acrobatics, for the only way to escape from the recurring thorns of climbing roses is to push oneself still further into the plant which, from the top of a step ladder is not easy. However climbing plants did not evolve to make life difficult for gardeners: they sacrificed stout stems in favour of thin scrambling ones as a means of getting to the light through the scaffolding provided by their stouter stemmed brethren. The term 'wall plant' has no botanical significance: it is a horti-cultural term applied generally to those plants which require the shelter provided by a wall or the convenience of a wall to lean on, or simply the plants which we choose to fasten to walls as espaliers, fans and other trained forms. Wall plants in general require very little support and, if planted first, provide just the scaffolding which climbers require, obviating the need for masses of wire.

Furthermore there is no reason why the scrambling nature of many climbers should be confined solely to other plants growing against walls. Many early-flowering herbaceous plants can be politely concealed and many shrubs enlivened by the growing of climbers whose flowers harmonize with those of the shrub or flower at another time to extend the season of interest. Care must be taken to match the vigour of the supported to that of the supporter and to avoid smothering plants of good form with a tangled mass of stems but the potential of climbers to enhance a garden on walls, wall plants and else-where is enormous.

As house prices climb and the size of gardens diminishes we are rapidly approaching the situation in which the surface area of the house, fences and other structures exceeds that of the soil surface which we habitually call the garden. Very clearly then making the most of your garden requires consideration of these vertical surfaces as potential vegetation carriers. Climbers on fences provide better enclosure in a smaller space than do shrubs and trees; climbers on pillars provide easily controlled height in the planting and climbers on a light overhead framework provide cool dappled shade in gardens too small to admit of overhead tree canopy. Even without the excuse of a small garden there are few domestic buildings of which the architecture could not be enhanced by the use of suitable wall plants – and there are a great many whose non-architecture warrants wholesale submersion in greenery.

The range of wall plants is enormous, indeed there are few shrubs which can not be grown against a wall of suitable orientation. To list just a few however, one would have to include the early-flowering *Azara dentata* and the hardier *A. microphylla*, both with sweetly scented yellow flowers, the beautiful blue Californian Lilacs, especially *Ceanothus dentatus* 'Impressus' for early summer and the many pyracanthas or firethorns laden with orange-yellow or red fruits in autumn and into the winter. *Pyracantha* can be grown quite satisfactorily on north facing walls. All form a framework of main stems with abundant young growth which can be cut back after flowering, except that *Pyracantha* is pruned in spring to retain its fruits as long as possible.

Two other plants worthy of mention

Caenothus impressus (right) and *Clematis montana* 'Rubens' can provide support for later-flowering climbers

are *Abutilon megapotanicum* and *Coronilla glauca*. Both are rather tender and definitely require protected situations and neither grows tall enough as a rule to support climbers but that is hardly a fault as neither of them is without flower long enough to merit plants of other seasons being grown upon them. The *Coronilla* has bright yellow flowers on a loose silver-grey bush, not long lived but easily replaced from seed. The *Abutilon* flowers are quite delightful – a puff of red turban with a flared yellow skirt beneath. It is scarcely ever to be seen without flowers on it in generous quantities.

Climbers fall into three categories, those capable of clinging to brick and similar rough surfaces, those which twine their whole beings around their supports and those which cling by tendrils or petioles.

The first group includes the many types of ivy, *Hedera* the *Parthenocissus* (Boston ivy and Virginia creeper) and climbing *Hydrangea*. These should not be grown on crumbling brick or stone walls as they can fall away taking the wall with them and ivy can push brick-work apart as its thick roots invade old mortar joints. They cannot be removed easily for pointing the wall but, on sound surfaces not in need of such treatment they are excellent plants. The range of ivies is enormous, varying in leaf colour, size and shape but all are slow growing initially, displaying their fine foliage in silhouette against the wall, then accelerate to cover large areas. If grown on free standing walls

Hedera colchica 'Variegata' is particularly cheerful in the winter. It will gradually clothe walls, stumps or the ground

149

they change form at the top to produce rounded leaved, flowering plants which are first class for cutting. *Partheno-cissus* and roof-tiles are deadly enemies but if the former are confined to the walls of a house (no easy task as both Boston ivy and Virginia creeper are very vigorous) they form attractive covers. I prefer the looser effect and brilliant crimson autumn colour of Virginia creeper (*Parthenocissus quinque-folia*) but the leaves fall very much earlier than those of Boston ivy *P. tricuspidata*. The latter stays close to the wall, the overlapping leaves imitating tile hangings and turning rich shades of red and purple late in the year, especially late if in shade. *Hydrangea petiolaris* forms a deeper layer of vegetation than the others as its short flowering shoots are up to half-metre (2 ft) long. The orange bark and dried inflorescences are attractive in winter so this is an excellent plant especially for north walls, except that it takes some years to become settled into the routine of flowering.

The twining plants, of which honey-suckle *Lonicera* and *Wistera* are most widely known, are difficult to use as they are unable to wind around large supports such as pergola posts and un-suitable for sending through wall plants which they will eventually strangle. However, a few strands of strong wire are sufficient for the first growths which in turn act as supports for later shoots. To be seen at its best *Wistera* needs to be kept firmly in hand, cutting back all long new shoots to about six leaves in summer and then almost to the base after leaf fall. Given such treatment it forms a sculptural group of spurs garlanded in long racemes of scented flowers. I must confess, however, that our *Wistera*, which came to us in a neglected state with a neglected house, gained the upper hand completely while the house was put into good repair and has managed thus far to stay ahead. It has huge pieces cut off when the roof is threatened or when gales bring the whole plant to the ground and we look forward to seeing it firmly disciplined next year – or the year after – or. . . ? Its punishment is postponed because it flowers freely despite the neglect and there are so many more important jobs. Honeysuckle is best left to itself with an occasional massacre. Our first attack on it yielded a rich harvest of layers rooted into well-rotted black leafmould in our gutters! Since then its activities have been curtailed but not suppressed and it forms a tangled mass outside the kitchen door, an ideal home for the blackbirds and *Clematis jackmanii* which roost there. A much smaller twiner is *Convolvulus althaeoides*. It takes courage to introduce bindweed into the garden but *C. althaeoides* is a welcome intro-duction with silver foliage becoming more and more deeply dissected as the stem elongates and bearing at each node one or two deep pink funnels. It is not a blaze of colour but flowers for most of the summer and struggles up to a metre (3 ft) high. Ours has less opportunity as it is planted in a new lavender hedge where its foliage is largely unnoticed while its flowers harmonize with those of the lavender, but as the latter fades the *Convolvulus* colonizes its flower stems and shows its more silver and more elegant foliage with great charm.

Mention of *Clematis* x *jackmanii* above brings me to the third and most useful group, clinging by tendrils or petioles. *Clematis*, of course, immediately spring to mind. Such is the variety and utility of the genus that whole books have been written on them and I would recommend reading any one of them for a much more adequate treatment than can be given here. That by Christopher Lloyd is especially useful, as indeed are all his books. In brief and breathless summary, however, the important points to remember are water, wilt and pruning. When trying to persuade *Clematis* to scramble through other plants, a purpose for which they are eminently suited, one must bear in mind that the other plant was there first and has probably fully exploited the soil. Thorough preparation is therefore necessary before admitting the *Clematis* and copious watering is required until establishment is evident. Wilt is a mysterious and incurable disease despite which *Clematis* are worth growing. It affects mainly large-flowered hybrids and there is some suggestion that deep planting, although not preventing the disease, will allow the plant to regenerate from below soil level if stricken. Pruning sounds complicated but can be vastly simplified by assuming that the most useful *Clematis* are those which

flower in late summer thus covering the unsightly remains of delphiniums or brightening the many earlier-flowered shrubs. As all the late-summer flowered *Clematis* are pruned by cutting very hard back in late winter, complicated pruning instructions are avoided. Late summer-flowering types include my favourite, the delicate-looking but vigorous *C. viticella* and its forms, the world's favourite *C.* x *jackmanii* and such large flowered hybrids as 'Jackmanii Alba' (white), 'Lady Betty Balfour' (purple) and 'Mme. Jules Corrévon' (nearly red). The yellow flowered *C. tangutica* and thick-sepalled *C. orientalis* also come into this group.

Clematis viticella deserves close inspection. It flowers from July sometimes into October

151

Clematis are not the only climbers, however. The Passion flower *Passiflora caerulea* is much hardier than is generally supposed and in reasonable summers will provide a bonus of bright yellow-orange fruits in addition to its beautiful and fascinating flowers. It is really too vigorous to grow through other plants and too subdued a colour to display its flowers well in such conditions so is best grown alone on wires. *Eccremocarpus scaber*, on the other hand, is a much less vigorous climber with clusters of bright, orange flowers in late summer and is ideal for growing through other, especially dark-leaved, plants. It can be grown as a half-hardy annual but will survive most winters in sheltered situations. Grapes are not noted for brilliant flowers although the small green flowers of the edible grape, *Vitis vinifera* are sweetly scented. They have other highly desirable attributes, however. The best adjective for *Vitis coignetiae* is 'overwhelming', and overwhelmed will be any small plants in its path. However, given a moist soil and an adequate expanse of pergola, fence, shed or large tree it will grow at a tremendous pace producing enormous leaves which colour brilliantly in autumn. Less vigorous and therefore often more useful is the edible grape, *Vitis vinifera*. Whether the grape is getting hardier or our climate warmer I do not know but there are now several commercial vineyards in Britain. The benefit of leafy shade, sweetly scented flowers and delicious fruit merit serious consideration in any garden with a

south-facing wall. *V. v.* 'Brandt' has only small fruits but the leaves are rich purple in the autumn and very beautiful.

One exceedingly beautiful climber which differs from all those previously mentioned in having no permanent superstructure is *Tropaeolum speciosum*. It is herbaceous and I mention it with some misgivings for it is one of the difficult plants, like *Berberidopsis*, *Lapageria* and *Crinodendron* which require warmth and high humidity. They flourish in the humid regions of the west coast but I wonder for how much longer I can resist attempting to grow the *Tropaeolum* on our much too dry and much too alkaline soil for its long streamers of neat compound leaves, brilliant scarlet flowers and turquoise fruits. *Berberidopsis corallina* has already found its way into the garden and is not only surviving but has produced one flower – so there is hope.

The genus *Tropaeolum* also includes the annual nasturtiums, some of which are good climbers but rather vigorous and much too attractive to blackfly. For the gardener interested in ornamental salads there is the compensating point that he, as well as the blackfly, can enjoy the mustard-flavour of young leaves. Much more slender is the half hardy *T. peregrinum* (*T. canariense*), Canary creeper with fringed yellow flowers. Other half-hardy annuals include the low, scrambling *Thunbergia alata* (black-eyed Susan) with orange or yellow flowers having a distinct black centre, the twining *Ipomoea violacea* (morning glory) and the tendril-

Eccremocarpus scaber, a half-hardy annual or doubtful perennial, is ideally suited to draping over dark greens

153

clinging *Cobaea scandens* with violet bell-shaped flowers. All are most satisfactorily grown by sowing the large seeds individually or in small groups in paper pots to germinate under glass and planting out the whole pot in June. *Thunbergia* will only do well in warm summers.

Sweet pea is another climber to which whole books have been devoted (and probably whole lives). For exhibition flowers one is recommended to lash single-stemmed plants to telegraph poles stood in several cubic yards of permanently moistened well rotted manure. Where plants and gardens are more important than flowers, however, very satisfactory results can be achieved by treating by the method described for other annuals above or even, on the better soils, by sowing *in situ* in May. For those not interested in large flowers the new 'old-fashioned' sweet peas are worth trying for their superb fragrance.

Some climbers, such as grape and Passion flower are best seen and grown in isolation. Many others are ideal for growing over herbaceous plants or through shrubs, including wall plants and this perhaps is the most useful group for small gardens, the climber providing a layer or festoon of flowers over already established plants. Ideal for this are *Clematis*, *Eccremocarpus scaber* and in suitable climate *Tropaeolum speciosum*.

It is also possible, however, to grow climbers through other climbers. On one corner of our house, for example, the unruly *Wistera sinensis* referred to

Tropaeolum speciosum, a skyward herbaceous perennial with brilliant scarlet flowers and turquoise fruits

earlier grows with a red climbing rose. The *Wistera* flowers mainly in May but has sufficient resources left in June to associate with the red roses while the fresh green bulk of the *Wistera* absorbs and supports the rose stems in a way that no amount of wire and twine could do. Odd flowers continue on both plants for another month before the honeysuckle *Lonicera periclymenum* emerges from relative obscurity to flower profusely and sweetly on the surface. As *Clematis viticella* grows only a few yards away (of which more in the next chapter) it is but a matter of time before this will extend the flowering season into October.

At another corner (I think we have

six) honeysuckle reigns supreme in its season – I strongly suspect that it has intercepted our storm-drain system somewhere between the gutter and the soakaway – but also supports a flourishing *Clematis* x *jackmanii* with 'Paul's Lemon Pillar' rose growing through both. There may be better *Clematis* but we inherited this with the house and it will stay because the two plants go together in a way that I never dreamed pinky-peachy-yellow and purple would. After the rose, the honeysuckle begins, to be joined later by the *Clematis*, but there are considerable problems: one main stem of the honeysuckle has been allowed to grow behind the down-pipe threatening to tear it from the wall, but it is the stem which furnishes the flowers which garland one extensive wall of our neighbour's house. The only solution appears to be to dismantle and re-erect the gutter and down-pipe, to save the honeysuckle – and undoubtedly to delay curbing the *Wistera* for yet another year! In return our neighbour's wall threatens to endow us with yet more *Wistera* and some Virginia creeper. The latter is tolerated in small quantities for its autumn colour in long festoons from the top of the wall but the *Wistera* is firmly resisted. To be caught between *two Wistera* plants is more than I could

stand, especially as we are already faced with an over-vigorous *Clematis montana* at the other side of the kitchen door with a *Cotoneaster horizontalis* half cut away to allow a newly planted *Azara dentata* to establish itself. With luck *Clematis montana* will start our year off, followed closely by the *Azara dentata* with its scented yellow flowers, then the *Cotoneaster* (allowed to grow back as the *Azara* becomes established above it) and climbing rose. Honeysuckle, purple *Clematis* and the trails of Virginia creeper follow with the red fruits of *Cotoneaster* carrying the rich red of the last creeper on into the new year. All this on 6 m (20 ft) of wall and virtually no ground space, most of the plants finding homes in chinks between a path and the wall except the *Clematis* which shares a square foot of soil with an old rosemary sprawling over the paving.

Mixtures of climbers can be very profitable but there is one drawback. With one climber on one shrub the latter provides the necessary form. With a climber cocktail there is no form, they make instead a bulging tangle of stems which complicates pruning of the various individuals as well as looking dreadful when the veil of green disappears in late autumn. However, the advantages far outweigh the problems, and when that *Wistera* is pruned. . . !

Part Five By Way of Summary

Chapter 18

Some Recipes for Plant Combination

ONE piece of advice has been given to me so often that I am beginning to believe it. If you want to make your point – says the advice – you must tell people what you are going to tell them, then tell them, then tell them what you have told them. In the introduction to this book I outlined briefly the philosophy behind what was to follow. In the various

chapters which followed I hope I have adhered to that philosophy with only sufficient deviation to make the point clear. Now we come to the last chapter. I am flattered that you are still reading but concerned that I have dwelt too long on the ingredients of the garden and not enough on its composition. In this last chapter, therefore, I should like to summarize very briefly what has gone before and then to describe a few garden scenes which give me pleasure because of the way in which the plants are mingled, inspirations and experiments in the medium of the 'flowery mead'.

The garden is a place for growing plants but not *just* for growing plants: it has many purposes. As the end result of considering the orientation, the view, the soil and other multifarious influences one arrives with a plan – on paper, in the head or on the ground in various stages of refinement. There are open spaces for play, for relaxation, to expose a view; there are enclosing elements, the buildings, screens and walls; there may be a vegetable garden hidden from view or on display but in either instance an integral part of the garden. Finally, to give structure to the garden, to soften hard outlines and to decorate, there are areas labelled 'Planting'.

The fuchsia garden at Hidcote: a pattern of brick and box in winter, a carpet of scilla in spring (left) and simple blocks of fuschia in summer (right): simple but brilliant

To make the most of your garden, especially if it is a small garden, this planting should not be segregated into tight beds and borders nor into rockeries, shrubberies, herbaceous borders and season bedding displays. It should form one large and all-enveloping plant group. Evergreens are the most important constituents, chosen to form an intermingling mosaic from tall shrubs – if the size of the garden permits – to ground hugging carpets. Within and upon this green mosaic the fleeting colours of flowers can come and go according to season: bulbs to pierce the carpet, later to be engulfed by herbaceous plants and annuals, making way in their turn for autumn bulbs and the other slender plants of autumn.

It would have been possible to fill a book with examples of suitable plant groupings, possible but not desirable as gardens are unique creations, not to be picked from a book like wallpaper patterns. Instead I have concentrated on ingredients with – I hope – sufficient information on growth habit and timing that it is possible to develop as many recipes as there are gardeners.

The first two examples of plant cocktails are from Hidcote Manor in Gloucestershire: if anyone still needs persuading that garden structure and arrangement of plants are more important than the plants themselves then Hidcote is the place to go. Near the house is a large rectangle filled with the Welsh poppy *Meconopsis cambrica* and bluebells, a pale and harmonious combination of yellow, orange and mauvy-blue. The *Meconopsis* has a long flowering season and, as the bluebells fade, their place is taken by another long-flowering plant, *Viola cornuta* with much the same colouring as bluebell. *Geranium endressii* provides firmer hummocks of foliage in the foreground and its flowers extend the colour combination towards pink. This is a simple colour scheme and effective for at least three months. It would be interesting to sow pastel colours of *Calendula*, the pot marigold into the mixture to continue the orange and yellow into autumn and to use *Campanula lactiflora* or *Agapanthus* hybrids for blue, or perhaps to experiment with complete changes of colour scheme as the season progresses. Additions or no, the orange and blue garden remains the best example of complete intermingling of plants that I have seen.

The fuchsia garden shows what can be achieved in a simple processional scheme. Hedges and low box edges define and give the garden its firm outline. In spring the beds are carpeted with blue *Scilla* and, as the flowers fade and the foliage becomes less than desirable hardy fuchsias emerge to smother them. *Fuchsia magellanica* 'Versicolor' and *F.* 'Mrs Popple' provide interesting variations in foliage colour and then flower from late summer until hard frosts kill back the young growth.

A more complex mixture which I have not yet tried in full was brought to mind by a 1974 note from Roy Elliott in the Royal Horticultural Society's

journal recommending the growing together of bearded iris and tulips. The tulips, planted 25 cm (10 ins) deep to avoid disturbance when dividing the iris, push up between the iris rhizomes to flower in May. As the tulips fade and their foliage sets about dying in the typical melodramatic fashion of tulips, the young iris foliage emerges to obscure the scene and to present its own beautiful flowers in June. Two seasons of colour from one patch of ground – but it is possible to improve on this because iris foliage is often far from attractive in the latter part of the year and I can report on the success of concealing the blemishes by sowings of hardy annuals. *Clarkia*, candytuft (*Iberis*), cornflower (*Centaurea*) and clary (*Salvia horminum*) are not exotic or unusual but are easy to grow and are just the shades of pink, lavender, blue and white which seem appropriate for the aftermath of an iris garden. Why stop there? Mr Elliott attributes the success of his tulips to the thorough drying out created by root activity of the iris which sounds exactly the conditions which suit the beautiful *Nerine bowdenii*, flowering in October. If one were greedy, one could bring in the old faithful *Crocus tommasinianus* to flower in February, a mixture of tulips for April and May, the iris for June, annuals in July and August to be pulled out in time for the emergence of *Nerine bowdenii*.

Three examples from our garden are chosen not to illustrate perfection, for in this our garden is sadly lacking, but

Tulips among the young leaves of irises which will produce colourful flowers in their turn
(copyright R. Elliot)

to describe three areas in which the planting is generous (to say the least!) and has been assembled to provide a long season of interest, with some success thus far and several failures.

The first is of about two square metres (2 sq yds) of earth and half square metre of path because *Hebe* 'Bowles Hybrid' which sprawls over half the area has not stopped short at the edge of the border. This *Hebe* of loose habit is not reproachful if cut hard back after flowering to keep it in bounds: indeed it will usually give a second crop of flowers as a sign of forgiveness. The foliage is excellent, evergreen with tinges of ever-purple even more pronounced in the stem and it flowers sporadically for most of the year. My favourite wallflower *Cheiranthus* 'Harpur Crewe' swells to encompass half the remaining area in its quite ordinary green leaves to be covered in spring with masses of strongly perfumed yellow flowers. Yellow with purple foliage may not sound attractive but it looks delightful: the *Hebe* is a distinctly red brand of purple and the wallflower might appropriately be described (in a chapter of recipes) as 'rich egg-yolk'. The bay formed between the two is filled with *Anthemis cupaniana*, a plant renowned for almost perpetual production of its large white daisies. In winter the anthemis foliage is grey-green and not always respectable but it is cut back to stumps each spring – the sprawling top growth provides an ample supply of cuttings – to encourage compact growth of its dissected silver leaves. If

treated in this way it forms an excellent foil for tulips. Otherwise the loose top growth forms rather too blanketing a blanket for the young tulip foliage. On the other side of the wallflower is a group of small herbaceous *Euphorbia* underplanted with *Iris reticulata*. The iris flowers in February or March, toning well with the *Hebe* then, as its foliage extends, the *Euphorbia* grows to support and eventually conceal it, forming a neat 15 cm (6 in) cushion of grey-green topped with long-lasting greenish-yellow flowers. Some autumn crocus (*C. speciosus* 'Artabir') planted to continue the floral season have been rather lost under the *Hebe* and succeed in producing only foliage, but I shall move them to the more open situation among the *Euphorbia* in front of the last plant in the group, *Kniphofia galpinii*. Thus permanent interest is provided by the foliage of *Hebe* and wallflower (both requiring regular curbing) and the sequence of flower is purple iris, wallflower, tulips, *Anthemis*. The foliage of *Anthemis*, *Euphorbia* and the grassy leaves of *Kniphofia* are added to the picture at this point with the flowers of *Hebe*. *Anthemis* continues to flower with the much less conspicuous *Euphorbia* and is eventually joined by *Kniphofia* and *Crocus*. Flowering is not continuous but this small piece of ground is seldom without a flower from February until October and is always attractively full and flourishing.

The second area is a larger 'L' shaped raised bed around an old well. Being on the corner between the front door and the main part of the garden, half seen from the main windows, it is an important area and, although less than two years old it has seen a great number of plants brought in and removed in the search for permanent beauty. Believing still that simplicity is necessary for areas viewed constantly at very close range the tip of the 'L' nearest the main windows contains only two plants, *Euonymus fortunei* 'Variegatus' and *Ajuga reptans* 'Atropurpurea'. The *Euonymus* is a graceful spreading shrub which effectively hides the rest of the bed during the winter and the cream variegation, almost white later in the year, contrasts well with the carpet of purple *Ajuga*. *Ajuga* is not truly evergreen but it remains presentable until long into the winter. Its colonies of upright blue flower-spikes are a great delight and the only care which this area has required since planting is the shearing off of the dead flower spikes and the occasional unleashing of a flower arranger to curb the spread of the *Euonymus*. The opposite corner of the bed is also planted with evergreens but in greater variety: *Helleborus foetidus* commands the entrace to the garden with *Bergenia cordifolia* next to it. Further along the edge thrift (*Armeria maritima*) and gold lace polyanthus almost completes the list of evergreens. The polyanthus has pride of place but this was a mistake. Its leaves in winter are green enough, but undistinguished so after flowering it will be divided and replanted more extensively in a more central position as the present distinc-

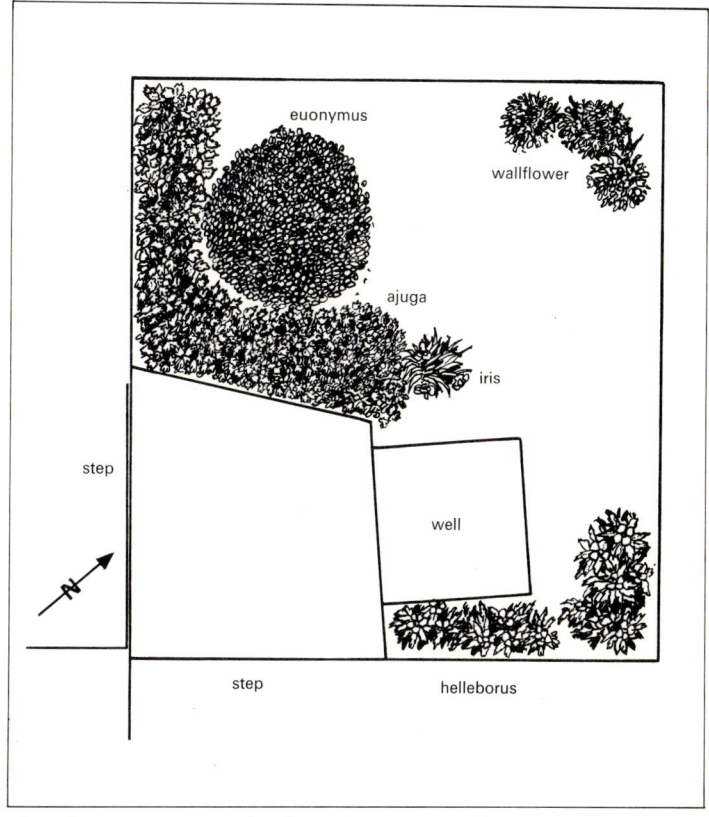

tion between marginal evergreens and central herbaceous plants is too rigid. This move will give the thrift an opportunity to expand and the latest acquisition for this bed, *Iris foetidissima* 'Variegata' will be moved (for the second time this year!) to join the thrift in this prominent position. *Iris foetidissima*, like *Helleborus foetidus* is not strictly evergreen but chooses early summer for its resting period and is therefore green (or green and white striped in the case of *I. f.* 'Variegata') throughout the winter. Its sword-shaped leaves provide an excellent contrast to the lower rounded evergreen plants and it appears to grow almost anywhere. The wallflower *Cheir-*

Evergreen plants in the 'Well Bed'

anthus 'Harpur Crewe' appears, once more, at the remaining corner of the bed as the last evergreen. It is interplanted with a dwarf Michaelmas daisy *Aster* which has similar though rather darker foliage. In the first summer the two plants combined well to form a big mound with yellow flowers in April and bright violet flowers in September but the Michaelmas daisy was a complete failure this year and will, I think, require annual division and replanting to keep it going in this very freely drained situation.

This evergreen planting on the toe, the very top and the bottom left-hand corner of the 'L' leaves a roughly triangular area for herbaceous plants and bulbs. *Brunnera macrophylla* features significantly, its early tall forget-me-nots being succeeded by large heart-shaped leaves which provide a good background for other flowers. The rest of the area is planted with winter aconite *Eranthis*, rather thinly at present but it usually thickens up quickly on our light soil. Violets have also seeded themselves in and will be allowed to remain. Daffodils appear after the aconites (the creamy white 'Beersheba' because they are seen against pink walls) followed closely by double red paeonies, polyanthus and the dwarf bearded *Iris* 'Green spot'. This was planted for its leaves but they are as unsatisfactory here as are the tall bearded iris after flowering. However, the young leaves are good, the flowers are excellent and a surrounding group of *Campanula portenschlagiana* quickly engulfs the re-

The 'well bed' in May: paeonies over the aconites with a skirt of campanulas for later interest

mains. The *Campanula* is a great success. Although not allotted any space for itself, it has spread around the *Bergenia*, under the paeony and *Helleborus* and over the dwarf iris to make a delightful informal edge flowering in July when the other plants are inactive. Summer is not the high season of this bed. It is leafy, with dappled shade from our unruly *Wistera* and quietly attractive with a few pelargoniums and *Chrysanthemum lutescens* tucked in where chinks can be found. In August, however, the white *Phlox* 'Mia Ruys' expands to fill the bed, followed by the dwarf Michaelmas daisy later on. Like the Michaelmas daisy the *Phlox* is also a candidate for annual division, not because it becomes exhausted but because it finds its feet and becomes rather too vigorous, especially too tall. Last year it was just the right height to be seen above the *Euonymus* from the main windows and to create a snowy peak to the planting. This year its height caused staking problems and the stemmy green gap between the *Eonymus* and *Phlox* flowers spoiled the effect.

There is no significance in the fact that our most recent trial ground is just the right size to accommodate a coffin: we have chosen the bonfire in preference to the compost heap as a means of disposing of our exhausted frames. However, it does help to emphasize that the new patch between our 'front' door and our 'back' door (geography is very confusing with an 'L' shaped semi-detached house) is very small for cultivation of nineteen species of plants.

The two mainstays of the border are *Pyracantha coccinea* and *Clematis viticella* which in themselves provide a long season of interest. The evergreen firethorn *Pyracantha* is trained flat against the wall. It is being rather brutally reduced from much larger dimensions and has not yet recovered sufficiently to flower and fruit with much freedom. The *Clematis* occupies a minute corner of the drive but spreads its rambling stems to the furthest point of the *Pyracantha* each year. It begins flowering in late July and continues into October. Although the flowers are dark purple, small and pendent, not a great blaze of colour from a distance, the effect in close-up is very elegant and as anyone approaching either door must pass within inches (or occasionally become completely entangled), a close-up view is assured. The flowers are even better seen against the white door. When the *Pyracantha* is established fully at its new size we may well consider the two plants to be enough but in the meantime the area provides a useful experimental site.

Despite the *Pyracantha*, other evergreens are important to define the informal edge of the border and ward off the many feet which pass daily to and fro. To one side, perennial candytuft *Iberis sempervirens* is planted; thrift *Armeria* peers out from the base of the *Pyracantha* and in the larger area to the left laced pinks *Dianthus* mark the corner with the ever-faithful *Bergenia* beside it for emphasis. Between the pinks and the wall a low dark green was required, open enough for *Cyclamen* to penetrate and we have chosen *Saxifraga* x *primulaize*. The dark green rosettes and airy pink spikes are miniature versions of London pride, their one disadvantage being that they are very loosely anchored. We have constantly to pick up rosettes thrown about by scavenging birds.

Behind the candytuft *Ceratostigma plumbaginoides* is underplanted with snowdrops, and a single clump of *Narcissus* 'Trevithian' (one of the most strongly perfumed *Narcissus*) is followed by a *Pelargonium*. This is a very sheltered, although not sunny corner and the *Pelargonium* usually continues to flower into November joined from early October by the purple leaves and blue flowers of *Ceratostigma*.

At the other end of the border three tall plants are surrounded by several smaller ones. *Iris sibirica*, *Anemone hupehensis* var. *japonica* and on early red chrysanthemum are very closely spaced. The iris flowers first and its slender foliage is very attractive for most of the summer. It grows rapidly for such a confined area and will need replanting every three years if all the other plants are not to be expunged. Japanese anemone is a splendid plant for finding its way between others and has no difficulty in surviving beneath the iris and flowering abundantly in autumn. The chrysanthemum may have a limited life in this border. It grows rather too tall and becomes entangled in the anemone flowers, spoiling their poise. I shall try cutting it hard back

in early summer to encourage shorter growth and if this fails then frequent renewal from cuttings may provide the answer. Its flowering with the white anemone is an asset as I prefer to have a balanced composition of flowering plants rather than one at a time but if it proves unmanageable by reasonable means it will be replaced either by a dahlia or by a *Kniphofia*. The latter is more probable since dahlias tend to be too large and leafy for the well-being of neighbouring plants and this is a very small area for constant upheavals. A *Kniphofia* would mean a temporary change of colour scheme from the red, white, pink, blue but as it would be flowering only with *Anemone* and *Ceratostigma* the change might be welcome especially as the backdrop is of dark green *Pyracantha* and white paintwork rather than the usual pink walls. The small forms of *Kniphofia* are very much neglected which is surprising as everyone seeing the few we have collected is very keen to grow them.

The smaller plants in this part of the border are *Primula* 'Wanda', a very low magenta *Primula* which objects not a bit to total submersion beneath anemones later in the year, the dwarf chrysanthemum known as 'Little Silver Princess' (but ascribed variously to *C. maximum* and *C. leucanthemum*) and *Cyclamen*. The chrysanthemum becomes taller with age but, like many plants, can be kept down by frequent division. It has very dark foliage to complement the flowers and this year has bloomed prolifically in December (but so have *Brunnera*, winter aconites *Eranthis* and witch hazel *Hamamelis*). The *Cyclamen* grow at the base of the *Clematis* with nothing more vigorous than *Saxifraga* x *primulaize* to compete with. The 'soil' is mainly tarmacadam and gravel but *Cyclamen hederifolium* seems to thrive in such conditions and seedlings rescued from the edge of the drive have already begun to flower.

More valuable will be *Cyclamen coum* when the one corm planted this year begins to flower. It is a truly winter flower, December and January, and is usually red so it will show up in splendid isolation against the white door and gravel surround. Violets have also seeded into this part of the garden so the isolation of *Cyclamen coum* may not be so complete.

Japanese anemone and outdoor chrysanthemums with a backdrop of pyracantha

Chapter 19

Epilogue

NONE of the schemes which I have described in this garden (which we acquired less than five years ago) relies on rare or difficult plants or on massive expenditure of time or money – neither of which we have in vast quantity. Indeed the oldest of the three schemes is only three years old and the others one and two years old. None of them is perfect, and even as I have been writing about them new ideas have occurred which I shall be trying as soon as possible. This change and experimentation is essential and it need involve no more effort than is grudgingly given to maintaining an unsatisfactory garden.

In all walks of life how much better it would be if people enjoyed putting a little thought and care into their activities rather than grudgingly doing as little as possible leaving their minds free to ponder on the supposedly greener grass in the other man's garden. If, by thinking in print about the pleasure I derive from gardening I can persuade one other person to look upon his garden as an asset instead of a chore then the book will have justified its existence. It is not work but care which enables each of us to make the most of our garden.

Index